Best Editorial Cartoons of the Year

ROY PETERSON
Courtesy Vancouver Sun

BEST EDITORIAL CARTOONS OF THE YEAR

2006 EDITION

Edited by
CHARLES BROOKS

PELICAN PUBLISHING COMPANY
GRETNA 2006

The cartoons in this volume are produced with the expressed
permission of the individual cartoonists and their respective
publications and/or syndicates. Any unauthorized
publication is strictly prohibited.

Library of Congress Serial Catalog Data

Best Editorial Cartoons, 1972-
Gretna [La.] Pelican Pub. Co.
v. 29 cm annual-
"A pictorial history of the year."

1. United States-Politics and government—
1969—Caricatures and cartoons—Periodicals.
E839.5B45 320.9'7309240207 73-643645
ISSN 0091-2220   MARC-S

Printed in Canada
Published by Pelican Publishing Company, Inc.
1000 Burmaster Street, Gretna, Louisiana 70053

Contents

Award-Winning Cartoons

2005 PULITZER PRIZE

NICK ANDERSON

Editorial Cartoonist
Louisville Courier-Journal

Born in Toledo, Ohio, 1967; graduated from Ohio State University, 1991; winner of the Charles M. Schulz Award for the best college cartoonist, 1989; editorial cartoonist for the Louisville *Courier-Journal,* 1991 to the present; also previous winner of the John Fischetti Award and the Sigma Delta Chi Award; syndicated by the Washington Post Writers Group since 1996; the names of his sons, Colton and Travis, are imbedded in all of his cartoons.

2004 JOHN FISCHETTI AWARD
(Selected in 2005)

CLAY BENNETT

Editorial Cartoonist
The Christian Science Monitor

Born in Clinton, South Carolina, 1958; graduated from the University of North Alabama, 1980; editorial cartoonist for the St. Petersburg *Times,* 1981-1994, and *The Christian Science Monitor,* 1998 to the present; previous winner of the Sigma Delta Chi Award, the National Headliner Award (three times), and the Pulitzer Prize.

2004 SIGMA DELTA CHI AWARD
(Selected in 2005)

JOHN SHERFFIUS

Editorial Cartoonist
jsherffius@aol.com

Born in Los Angeles, 1961; graduated from UCLA in 1984 and California State University, Northridge in 1986; editorial cartoonist for the *Orange Coast Daily Pilot,* 1990-1991, the *Ventura County Star,* 1992-1998, and the St. Louis *Post-Dispatch,* 1998-2003; also previous winner of the Scripps-Howard Award, the Robert F. Kennedy Award, and the National Press Foundation's Berryman Award.

2005 OVERSEAS PRESS CLUB AWARD

KEVIN KALLAUGHER

Editorial Cartoonist
The Baltimore Sun and *The Economist*

Graduated with honors from Harvard College in 1977; in 1978 became the first resident cartoonist in the 145-year history of the prestigious *Economist* magazine in London; editorial cartoonist for the *Baltimore Sun,* 1988 to the present; also previous winner of Overseas Press Club Award (twice), the Berryman Award, and the Feature Cartoon of the Year Award presented by the Cartoonist Club of Great Britain.

TOM TOLES

Editorial Cartoonist
The Washington Post

Born in Buffalo, New York; graduated from the University of New York at Buffalo; editorial cartoonist for the Buffalo *Courier-Express,* 1973-1982, the *Buffalo News,* 1982-2002, and the *Washington Post,* 2002 to the present; selected by Editor and Publisher as Editorial Cartoonist of the Year, 2002; also previous winner of the John Fischetti Award, the Free Press Association Mencken Award, and the Global Media Award; syndicated by Universal Press Syndicate.

2004 SCRIPPS-HOWARD AWARD
(Selected in 2005)

STEVE SACK

Editorial Cartoonist
The Minneapolis Star-Tribune

Born in St. Paul, Minnesota; editorial cartoonist for *The Minnesota Daily,* 1978, the Fort Wayne, Indiana, *Journal Gazette,* 1979-1981, and the *Minneapolis Star-Tribune,* 1981 to the present; previous winner of the Sigma Delta Chi Award and the National Headliner Award.

2004 NATIONAL NEWSPAPER AWARD / CANADA
(Selected in 2005)

THEO MOUDAKIS

Editorial Cartoonist
The Toronto Star

Born in Montreal, Quebec, in 1965; editorial cartoonist for the *Halifax Daily News,* 1991-2000, and the *Toronto Star,* 2000 to the present.

Prime Minister Paul Martin, who suffered a no-confidence vote by the House of Commons in late November

Best Editorial Cartoons of the Year

ED HALL
Courtesy Baker County Press

14

The Bush Administration

Condoleezza Rice was sworn in as the first black female secretary of state, and, over fierce opposition, John Bolton was confirmed as ambassador to the United Nations. After Justice Sandra Day O'Connor announced her retirement from the U.S. Supreme Court and Chief Justice William Rehnquist died following an extended illness, President Bush found himself with two Court nominations. To replace Rehnquist, he named John Roberts, a former White House lawyer, who was easily confirmed.

But Bush's nomination of longtime friend Harriet Miers for the other court seat provoked a revolt among his supporters. She withdrew, and Bush then nominated an experienced jurist, Sam Alito, who was immediately attacked as being too far to the right. Hearings on his nomination were scheduled to begin in January.

Lewis "Scooter" Libby, Vice President Dick Cheney's chief of staff, was indicted on five counts of perjury, obstruction of justice, and making false statements in an investigation of the leak of a CIA operative's identity.

Several studies indicated that Americans believe they are safer today than five years ago but are critical of what they perceive as a failure to control the nation's borders. By late November, polls showed Bush's approval rating had dropped below 40 percent.

ROBERT ARIAIL
Courtesy The State (S.C.)

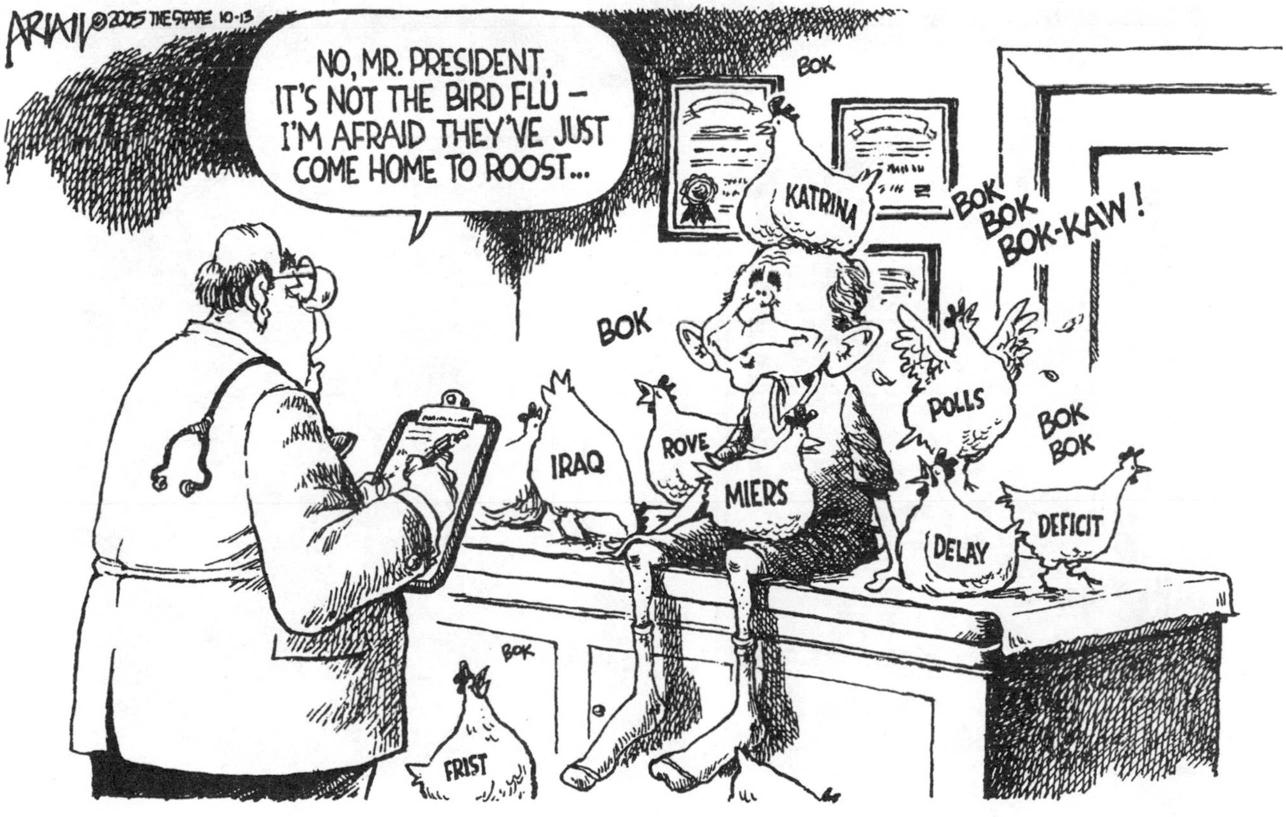
ARIAIL ©2005 THE STATE 10-13
NO, MR. PRESIDENT, IT'S NOT THE BIRD FLU – I'M AFRAID THEY'VE JUST COME HOME TO ROOST...
BOK
KATRINA
BOK BOK BOK-KAW!
BOK
POLLS
BOK BOK
IRAQ
ROVE
MIERS
DELAY
DEFICIT
BOK
FRIST

WALT HANDELSMAN
Courtesy Newsday

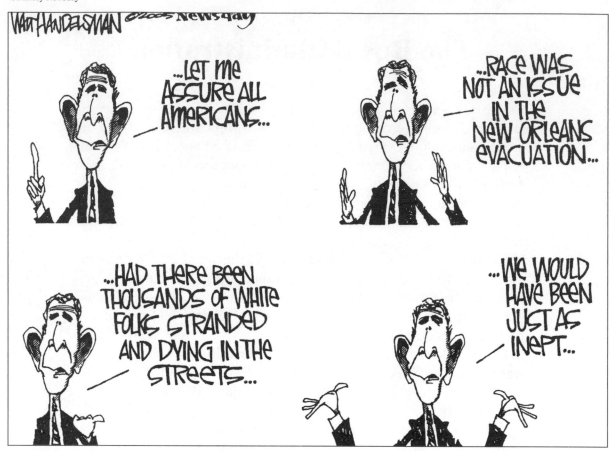

JOHN SHERFFIUS
Courtesy jsherffius@aol.com

MICHAEL RAMIREZ
Courtesy Los Angeles Times

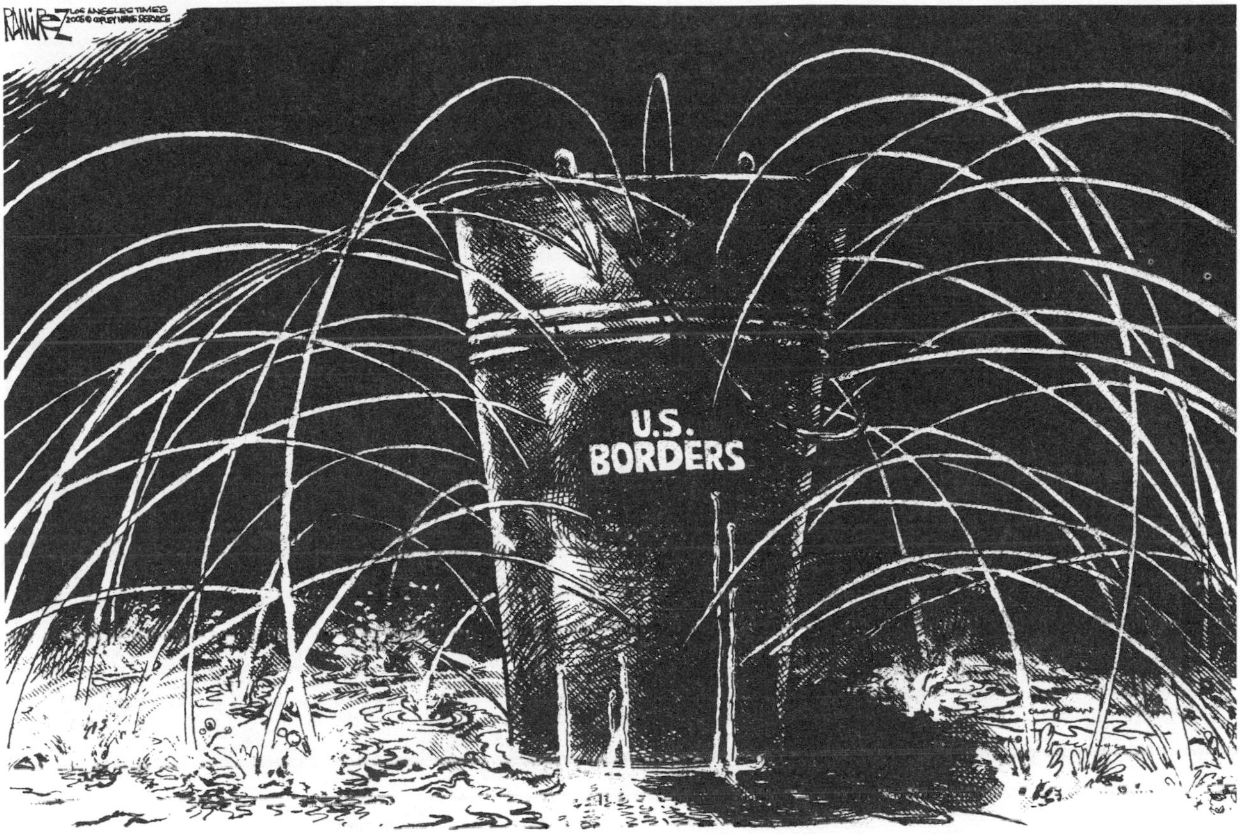
U.S.
BORDERS

SCOTT STANTIS
Courtesy Birmingham News

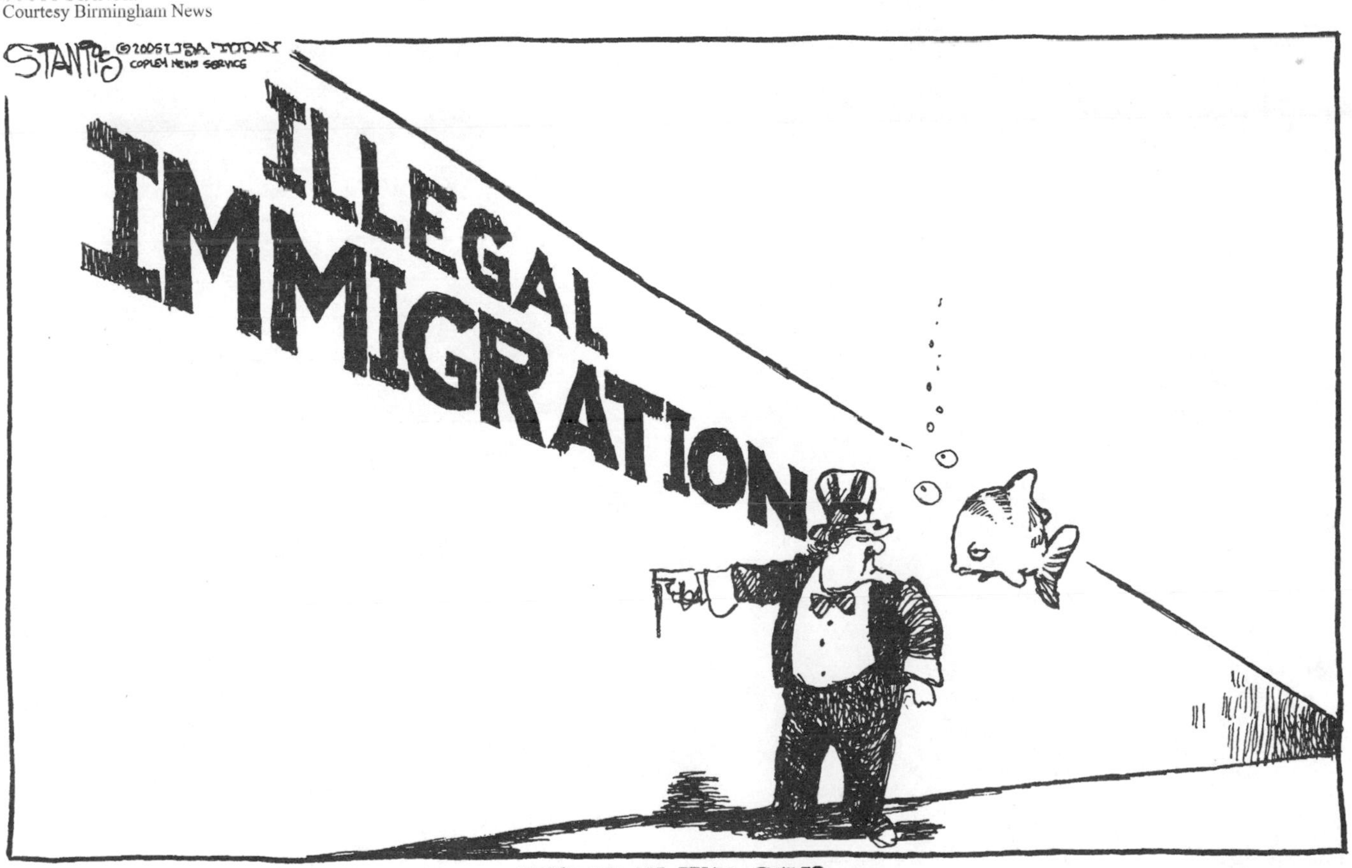
ILLEGAL
IMMIGRATION

FINGER IN THE DIKE

ROBERT ARIAIL
Courtesy The State (S.C.)

BOB GORRELL
Courtesy Creators Syndicate

JOHN RILEY
Courtesy johnrileycartoons.com

MIKE PETERS
Courtesy Dayton Daily News

VAUGHN LARSON
Courtesy The Review (Wisc.)

S. C. RAWLS
Courtesy Rockdale Citizen

BRIAN DUFFY
Courtesy Des Moines Register

STEVE SACK
Courtesy Minneapolis Star-Tribune

MARK THORNHILL
Courtesy North County Times (Calif.)

PAUL CONRAD
Courtesy Tribune Media Services
Used with permission

JERRY HOLBERT
Courtesy Boston Herald

22

POL GALVEZ
Courtesy Philippine News

JIM BORGMAN
Courtesy Cincinnati Enquirer

23

J. P. TROSTLE
Courtesy The Herald-Sun (N.C.)

BILL VALLADARES
Courtesy Montclair Times (N.J.)

NICK ANDERSON
Courtesy Louisville Courier-Journal

J. D. CROWE
Courtesy Mobile Register

STEVEN LAIT
Courtesy Oakland Tribune

JEFF DANZIGER
Courtesy NYTS/CWS

DICK LOCHER
Courtesy Chicago Tribune

ERIC SHANSBY
Courtesy Washington Post

FRANK CAMMUSO
Courtesy The Post-Standard

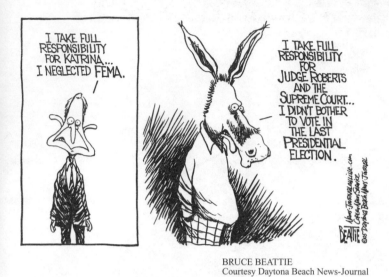

BRUCE BEATTIE
Courtesy Daytona Beach News-Journal

DAVID DONAR
Courtesy McComb Daily (Miss.)

ALAN VITELLO
Courtesy Greeley Tribune

BOB UNELL
Courtesy Kansas City Star

ROB ROGERS
Courtesy Pittsburgh Post-Gazette

JON RICHARDS
Courtesy Albuquerque Journal North

JOHN SHERFFIUS
Courtesy jsherffius@aol.com

Lies

FRANK CAMMUSO
Courtesy The Post-Standard

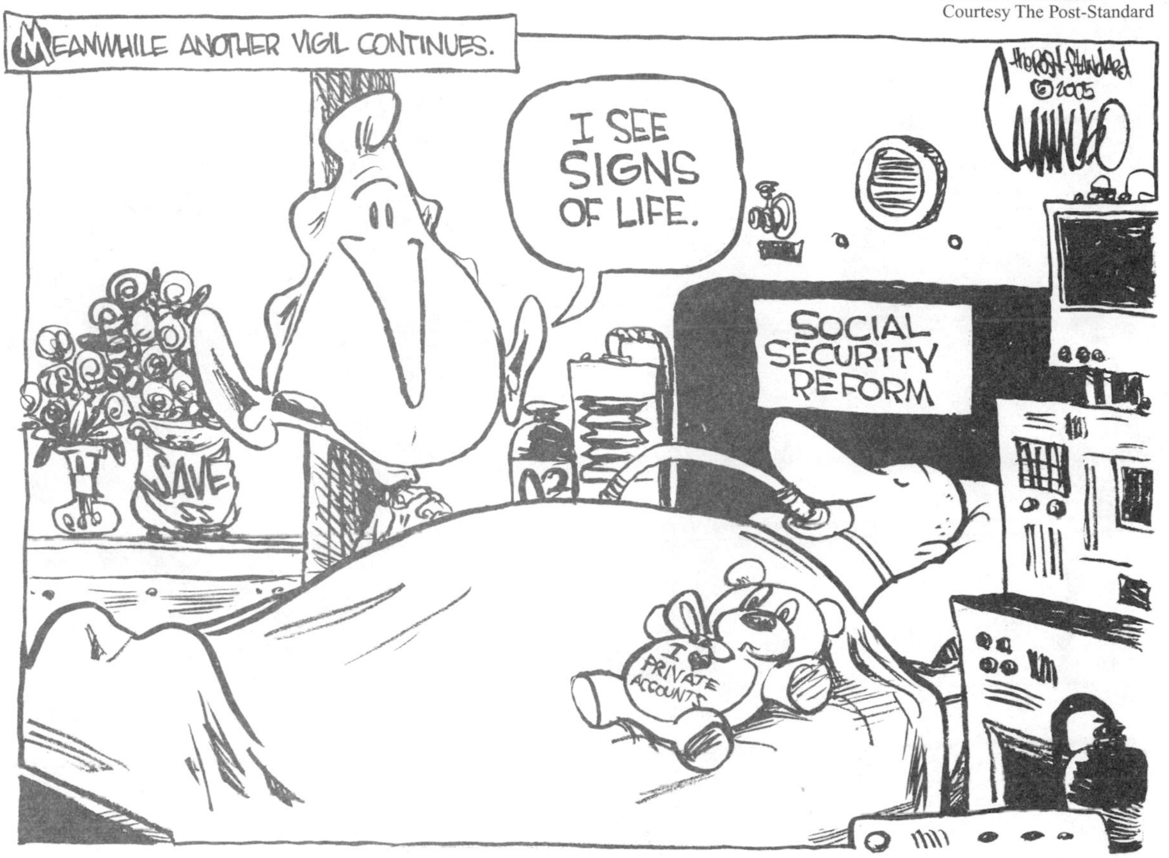

MEANWHILE ANOTHER VIGIL CONTINUES.
I SEE SIGNS OF LIFE.
SOCIAL SECURITY REFORM
SAVE SS
I ♥ PRIVATE ACCOUNTS
O2
The Post-Standard © 2005 CAMMUSO

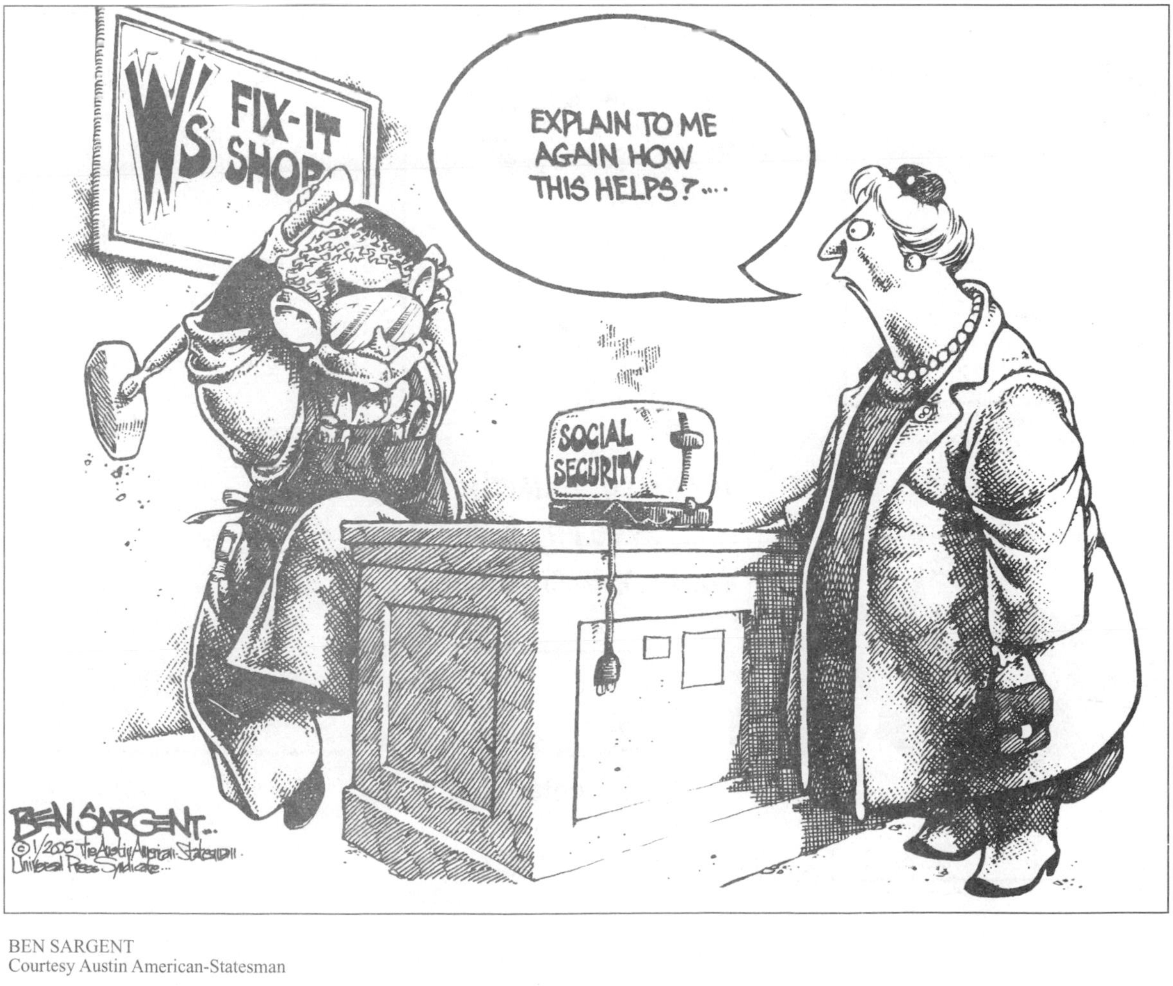

W'S FIX-IT SHOP
EXPLAIN TO ME AGAIN HOW THIS HELPS?....
SOCIAL SECURITY
BEN SARGENT

BEN SARGENT
Courtesy Austin American-Statesman

DAN CARINO
Courtesy Knight Ridder/Tribune
Information Services

PAUL CONRAD
Courtesy Tribune Media Services
Used with permission

DREW CHAPMAN
Courtesy CommentaryPage.com

STEVE SACK
Courtesy Minneapolis Star-Tribune

STAR TRIBUNE
SACK

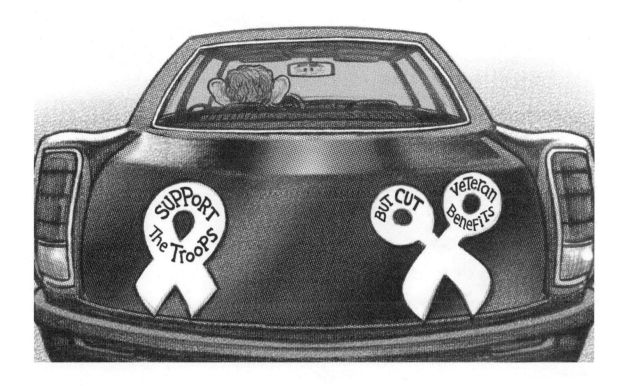

SCOTT-ALLEN PIERSON
Courtesy Viking News

THE EVOLUTION OF THE WHITE HOUSE

WALT HANDELSMAN
Courtesy Newsday

PEDRO MOLINA
Courtesy CWS

pxmolina@turbonett.com

JAMES CASCIARI
Courtesy Treasure Coast Newspapers

JEFF DANZIGER
Courtesy NYTS/CWS

JOHN BRANCH
Courtesy San Antonio Express-News

MIKE PETERS
Courtesy Dayton Daily News

DRAPER HILL
Courtesy Grosse-Pointe Publishing Co.

PAUL CONRAD
Courtesy Tribune Media Services
Used with permission

BOB GORRELL
Courtesy Creators Syndicate

ROB HARRIMAN
Courtesy Portland Tribune

JEFF PARKER
Courtesy Florida Today

BOB GORRELL
Courtesy Creators Syndicate

STEVE GREENBERG
Courtesy Ventura County Star

DANA SUMMERS
Courtesy Orlando Sentinel

JOEL PETT
Courtesy Lexington Herald-Leader

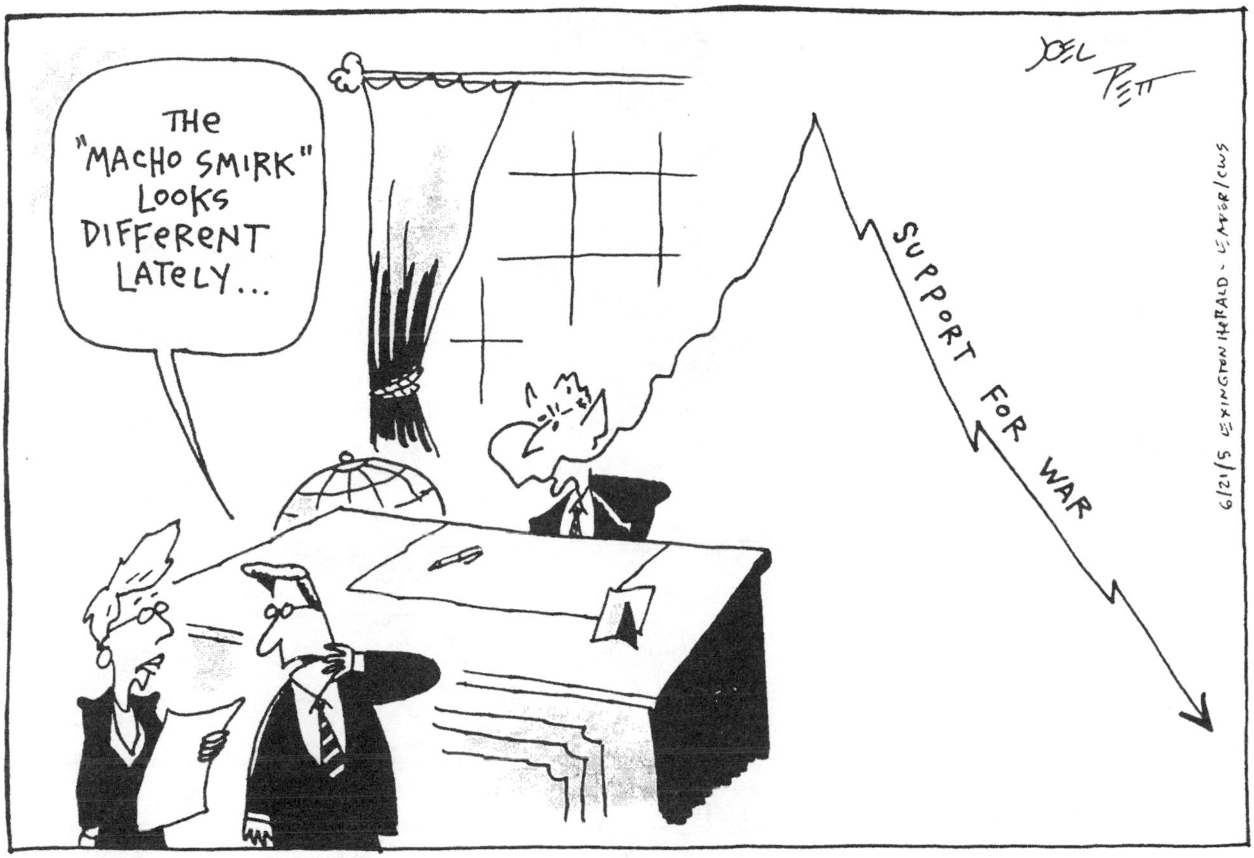
JOEL PETT
THE "MACHO SMIRK" LOOKS DIFFERENT LATELY...
SUPPORT FOR WAR

GARY MARKSTEIN
Courtesy Copley News Service

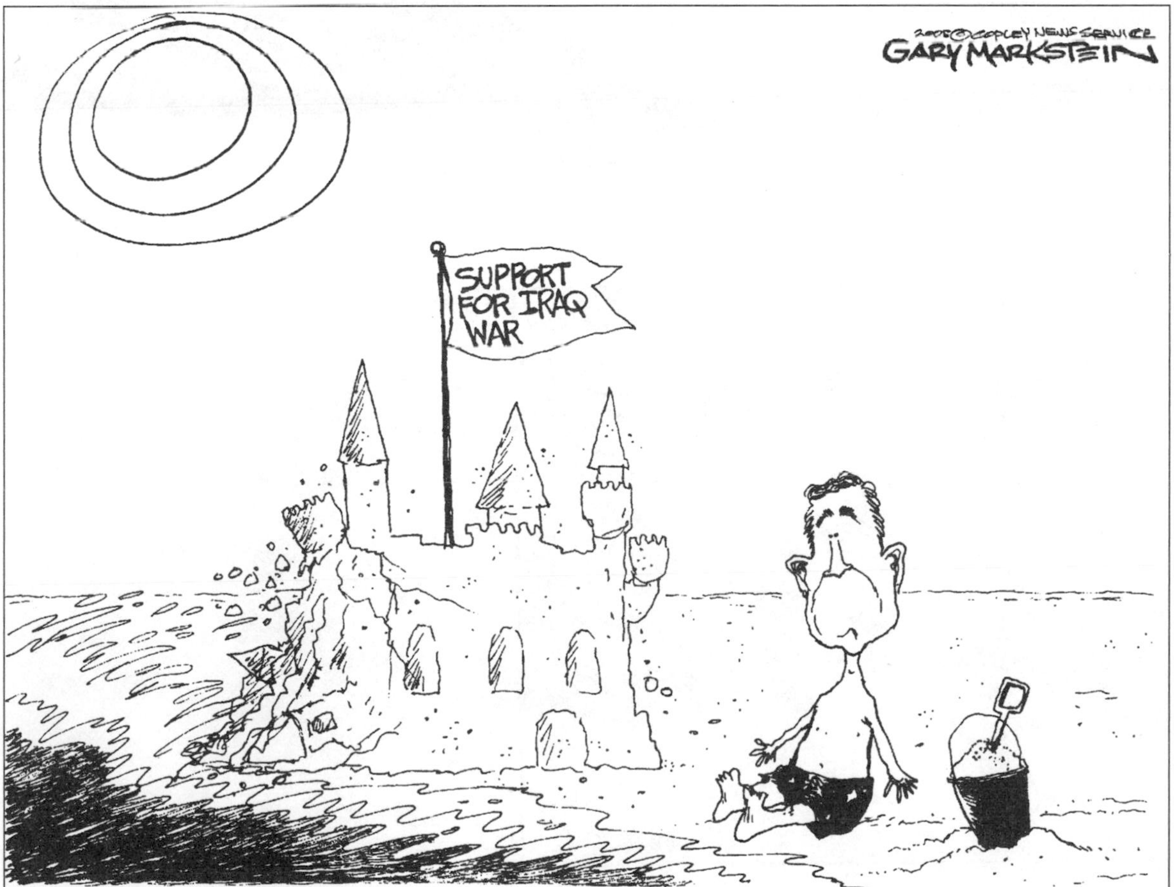
GARY MARKSTEIN
SUPPORT FOR IRAQ WAR

JEFF DANZIGER
Courtesy NYTS/CWS

TONY BAYER
Courtesy The News-Dispatch (Ind.)

STAN BURDICK
Courtesy Lake Champlain Weekly

PAUL CONRAD
Courtesy Tribune Media Services
Used with permission

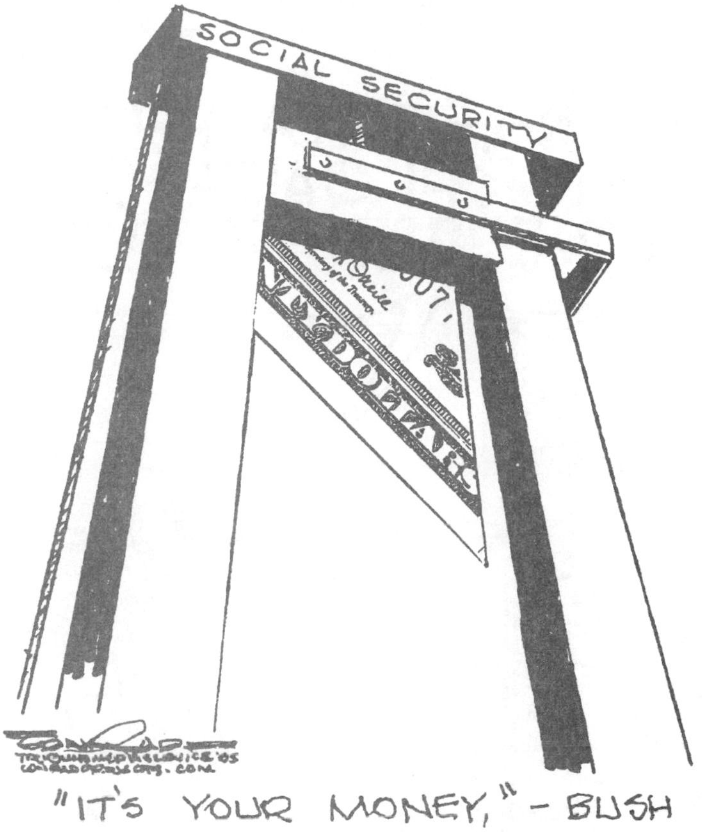
SOCIAL SECURITY
"IT'S YOUR MONEY," - BUSH

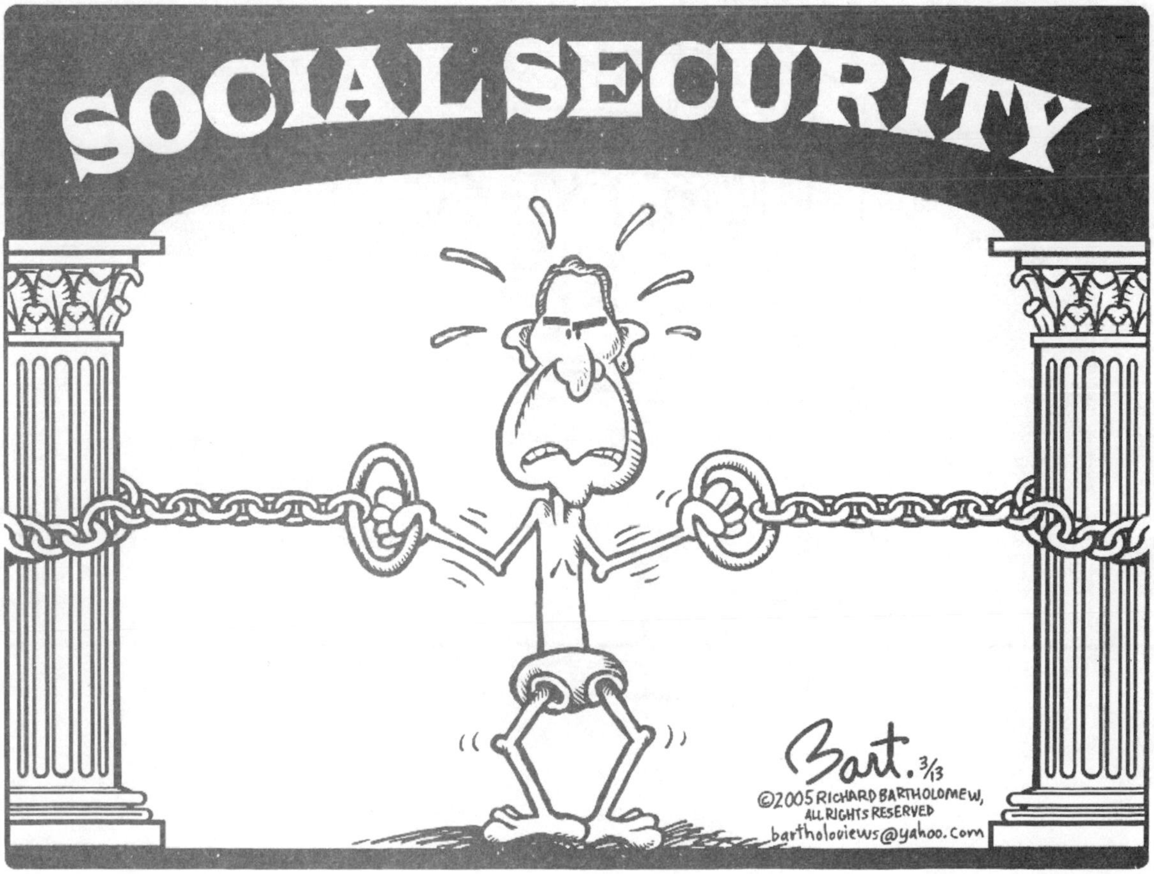
SOCIAL SECURITY
Bart. 3/13
©2005 RICHARD BARTHOLOMEW, ALL RIGHTS RESERVED
bartholoviews@yahoo.com

RICHARD BARTHOLOMEW
Courtesy bartholoviews.com

ANDY DONATO
Courtesy Toronto Sun

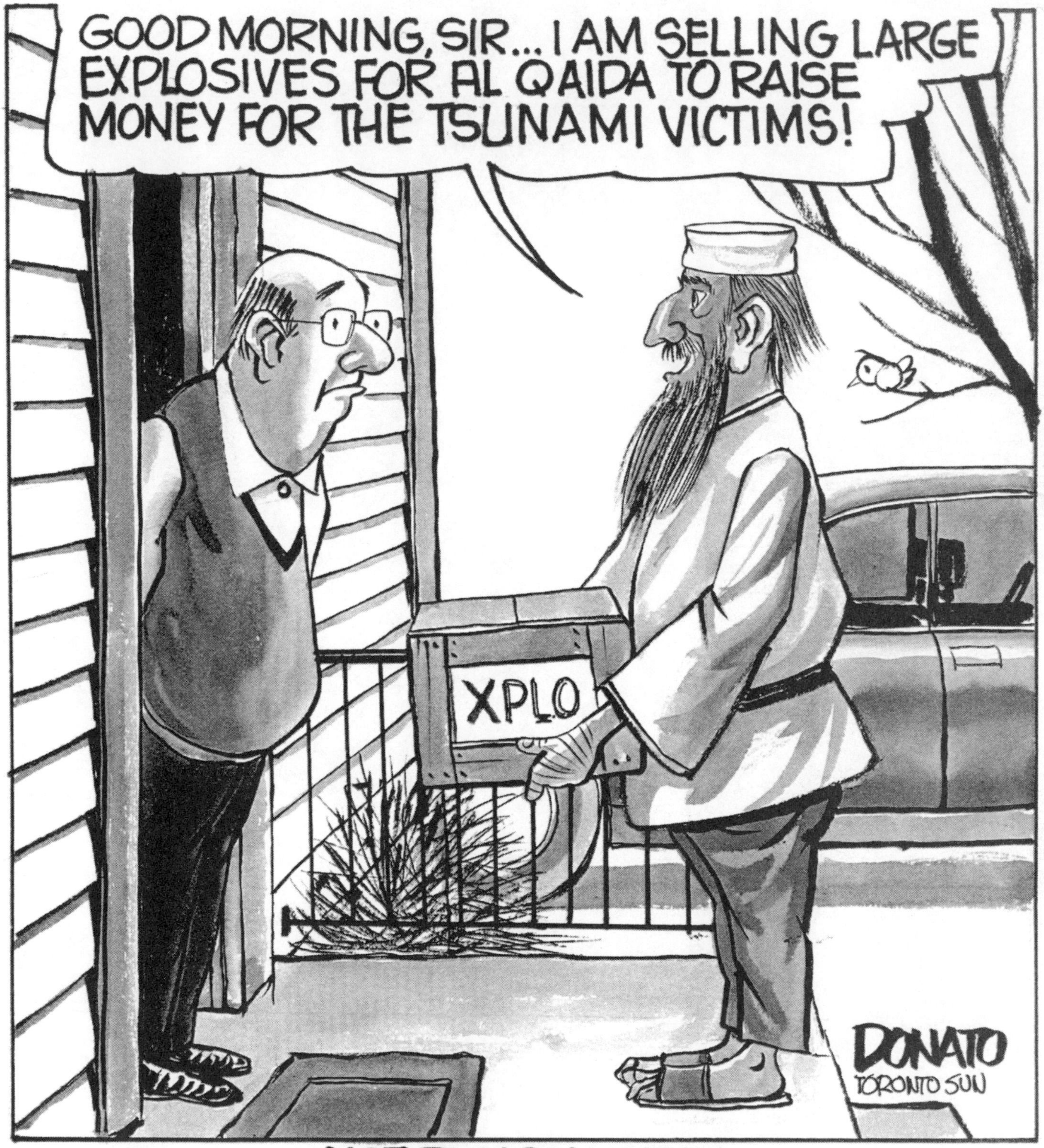
GOOD MORNING, SIR... I AM SELLING LARGE EXPLOSIVES FOR AL QAIDA TO RAISE MONEY FOR THE TSUNAMI VICTIMS!
XPLO
DONATO
TORONTO SUN

NOT BLOODY LIKELY

Iraq / Terrorism

Saddam Hussein's trial for crimes against humanity began late in the year following Iraq's first democratic elections. About 60 percent of the country's fourteen million voters defied terrorists and risked death to cast their ballots. In a second election, Iraqi citizens approved a new constitution despite widespread opposition by the Sunnis. The Shiites, the other major branch of Islam, generally cast their votes in support of a democratic government.

Allegations of the mistreatment of Iraqi prisoners at the hands of U.S. troops and Iraqi solders continued, and the FBI warned that terrorist sleeper cells could be operating in the United States. There was widespread belief that al-Qaida and other terrorist groups were continuing their efforts to obtain chemical, biological, and nuclear weapons.

Terrorists attacked London's subway system on July 7, killing 56, including the four suicide bombers. More than 700 were injured. A week later, a second series of subway and bus attacks failed, and many suspects were arrested.

Critics of the Bush Administration claimed that the deployment of National Guard troops in the war on terror undermined the nation's ability to deal with natural disasters such as Hurricane Katrina.

DICK LOCHER
Courtesy Chicago Tribune

KEVIN KALLAUGHER
Courtesy Baltimore Sun

MARK BAKER
Courtesy Army Times

JIM DYKE
Courtesy Jefferson City News-Tribune

JERRY HOLBERT
Courtesy Boston Herald

DOUG MacGREGOR
Courtesy Ft. Myers News-Press

BOB LANG
Courtesy Rightoons.com

BOB LANG © 10-18
RightToons.com
I WANT TO BE JUST LIKE HIM WHEN WE FINALLY VOTE FOR OUR PRESIDENT....
Z
IRAQI CHARTER VOTE
U.S. VOTERS
CHIPS

STEVE KELLEY
Courtesy The Times-Picayune (La.)

S.KELLEY THE TIMES-PICAYUNE ©2005
ABSOLUTELY NO BEHEADINGS WITHIN 100 FEET OF POLLS THANK YOU.
IRAQ ELECTION

BUNKER HILL MIDWAY INCHON
NORMANDY IRAQ BULL RUN
LEXINGTON SAN JUAN GULF
GETTYSBURG SAIPAN TET
ANZIO PEARL HARBOR BELLEAU WOODS BASTOGNE
OKINAWA GUADALCANAL PLOESTI SHILOH FT. WAGNER
KHE SANH IWO JIMA PUSAN CORAL SEA VALLEY FORGE

LOCHER ©2005 CHICAGO TRIBUNE

DICK LOCHER
Courtesy Chicago Tribune

JAMES CASCIARI
Courtesy Treasure Coast Newspapers

KEVIN KALLAUGHER
Courtesy Baltimore Sun

JIM LANGE
Courtesy Daily Oklahoman

PATRICK O'CONNOR
Courtesy Los Angeles Daily News

JERRY HOLBERT
Courtesy Boston Herald

SAD-DUMB and DUMBER

MIKE PETERS
Courtesy Dayton Daily News

DOUG MacGREGOR
Courtesy Ft. Myers News-Press

STEVE McBRIDE
Courtesy Independence Daily Reporter (Kan.)

GARY MARKSTEIN
Courtesy Copley News Service

STEVE LINDSTROM
Courtesy Duluth News-Tribune

S. W. PARRA
Courtesy Fresno Bee

ETTA HULME
Courtesy Ft. Worth Star-Telegram

THE STRATEGY FOR GETTING OUT OF IRAQ

NICK ANDERSON
Courtesy Louisville Courier-Journal

DOMINO THEORY

THE 2,000 AMERICAN SOLDIERS KILLED IN IRAQ

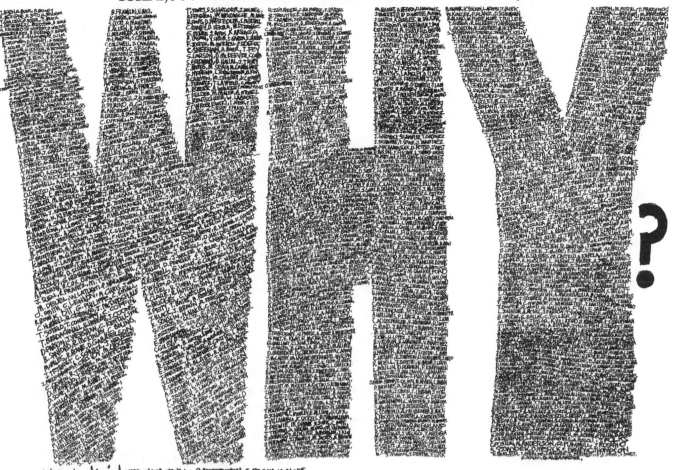

MIKE LUCKOVICH ATLANTA JOURNAL-CONSTITUTION © AJC.COM 10-26-05

MIKE LUCKOVICH
Courtesy Atlanta Journal-Constitution

BOB ENGLEHART
Courtesy Hartford Courant

55

JEFF STAHLER
Courtesy Columbus Dispatch

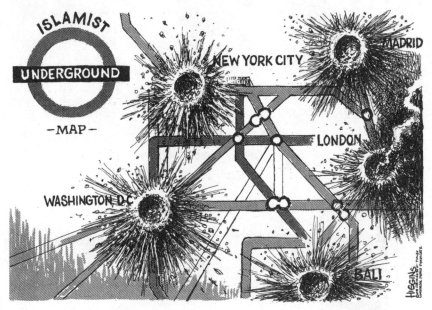

JACK HIGGINS
Courtesy Chicago Sun-Times

MIKE SCOTT
Courtesy Newark Star-Ledger

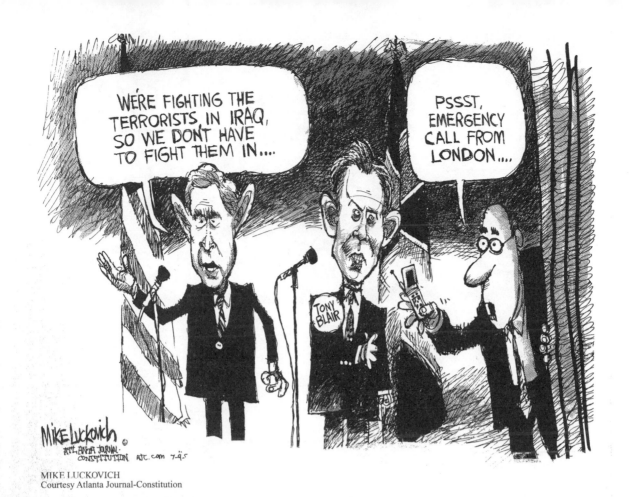

MIKE LUCKOVICH
Courtesy Atlanta Journal-Constitution

JIM BORGMAN
Courtesy Cincinnati Enquirer

GARY VARVEL
Courtesy Indianapolis Star

MARK BAKER
Courtesy Army Times

JONATHAN TODD
Courtesy Shreveport Times

VAUGHN LARSON
Courtesy The Review (Wisc.)

MICHAEL RAMIREZ
Courtesy Los Angeles Times

STEVE LINDSTROM
Courtesy Duluth News-Tribune

JIM BORGMAN
Courtesy Cincinnati Enquirer

"DESPAIR, VIOLENCE, CONSTANT DANGER.... NEW ORLEANS MUST BE HELL."

JEFF STAHLER
Courtesy Columbus Dispatch

MIKE LUCKOVICH
Courtesy Atlanta Journal-Constitution

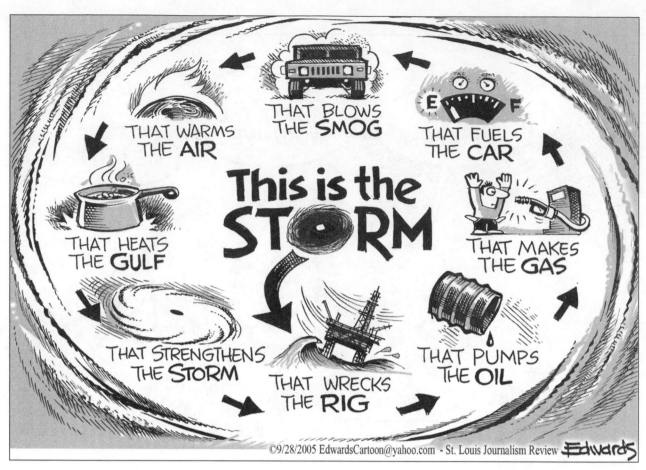

STEVE EDWARDS
Courtesy St. Louis Journalism Review

JACK HIGGINS
Courtesy Chicago Sun-Times

Natural Disasters

Natural disasters wreaked havoc throughout the world during 2005.

On August 29, Katrina, the strongest hurricane ever to strike the United States, devastated New Orleans and parts of the Mississippi Gulf Coast. Protective levees in New Orleans failed, allowing much of the city to be inundated. The death toll exceeded 1,000. Hurricane Rita, another Category 5 storm, followed Katrina, pummeling the Louisiana—Texas border. It was estimated that a rebuilding effort in the wake of the two storms would cost $200 billion. The big question remains: Who will pay for it?

Just about everybody was blamed for what the public perceived as an agonizingly slow and ineffectual response to the devastation. President Bush and the Federal Emergency Management Agency headed by Michael Brown drew a lion's share of the criticism. Many pointed fingers at Louisiana Gov. Kathleen Blanco and New Orleans Mayor Ray Nagin for not doing more, more swiftly, to assist the thousands of victims.

One of the worst natural disasters in the history of the world came at the end of 2004 in the form of a giant tsunami. Rising from an earthquake in the Indian Ocean, it battered eleven countries in Southeast Asia and took 150,000 lives. Late in the year, a 7.6-magnitude quake rocked Pakistan, killing more than 70,000.

ANDY DONATO
Courtesy Toronto Sun

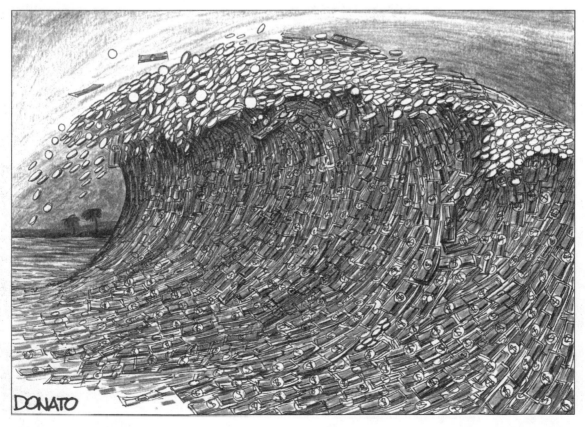

PETER EVANS
Courtesy Islander News (Fla.)

DOUG REGALIA
Courtesy Contra Costa Newspaper Group

BOB LANG
Courtesy Rightoons.com

JAKE FULLER
Courtesy Gainesville Sun

CRAIG TERRY
Courtesy Northwest Florida Daily News

MARK THORNHILL
Courtesy North County Times (Calif.)

RICK KOLLINGER
Courtesy The Star-Democrat (Md.)

BOB ENGLEHART
Courtesy Hartford Courant

BEN SARGENT
Courtesy Austin American-Statesman

SAGE STOSSEL
Courtesy The Atlantic Monthly

LINDA BOILEAU
Courtesy Frankfort State Journal

CLAY JONES
Courtesy The Free Lance Star (Va.)

ELIZABETH BRICQUET
Courtesy Kingsport Times-News

CHRIS BRITT
Courtesy State Journal-Register (Ill.)

DEB MILBRATH
Courtesy CNN AAEC

MIKE PETERS
Courtesy Dayton Daily News

CLAY JONES
Courtesy The Free Lance Star (Va.)

RICKY NOBILE
Courtesy Hattiesburg American

JOE MAJESKI
Courtesy Wilkes-Barre Times-Leader

GUY BADEAUX
Courtesy Le Droit (Can.)

RICHARD WALLMEYER
Courtesy Long Beach Press-Telegram

STEVE McBRIDE
Courtesy Independence Daily Reporter (Kan.)

DAN CARINO
Courtesy Knight Ridder/Tribune Information Services

STEVE KELLEY
Courtesy The Times-Picayune (La.)

BILL WHITEHEAD
Courtesy Kansas City Business Journal

HAP PITKIN
Courtesy Boulder Daily Camera

J. D. CROWE
Courtesy Mobile Register

ETTA HULME
Courtesy Ft. Worth Star-Telegram

ROBERT ARIAIL
Courtesy The State (S.C.)

S. C. RAWLS
Courtesy Rockdale Citizen

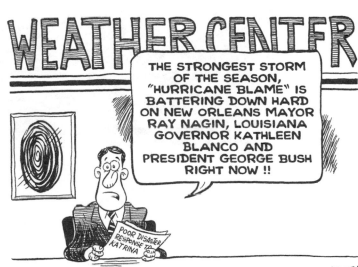

J. R. ROSE
Courtesy Byrd Newspapers of Virginia

ED GAMBLE
Courtesy Florida Times-Union

TIM BENSON
Courtesy The Argus-Leader (S.D.)

TOM STIGLICH
Courtesy The Northeast Times (Pa.)

Media / Entertainment

An aging Mark Felt, the No. 2 man in the FBI during Richard Nixon's presidency, revealed himself to be Deep Throat, the inside source that reporters Carl Bernstein and Bob Woodward used to help bring down Nixon in the celebrated Watergate investigation.

A *Newsweek* article alleged that interrogators at the U.S. military prison in Guantanamo Bay, Cuba, had flushed copies of the Koran down the toilet. After ensuing rioting killed 17 and the allegation was proved false, the magazine retracted the charge and apologized. As a result, Washington journalists began to reexamine the widespread use of unidentified sources. Many journalists contend that the practice of attributing so-called facts to unnamed sources has widened the media's credibility gap.

After a 14-week trial at midyear, rock star Michael Jackson was acquitted on all charges related to sexual misconduct with young boys at his Neverland Ranch. He was also reported to be millions of dollars in debt although spokesmen denied it.

Actor Robert Blake was acquitted of murder charges in the 2001 slaying of his wife, Bonny Lee Bakley. In a later civil case, however, he was ordered to pay Bakley's family $30 million.

Southern Baptists ended a longstanding boycott of Walt Disney productions.

JOSEPH F. O'MAHONEY
Courtesy The Patriot Ledger (Mass.)

ADAM ZYGLIS
Courtesy The Buffalo News

TIME MAGAZINE DECIDES TO REVEAL ITS SOURCES...

JIM HOPE
Courtesy Culpepper News (Va.)

AT THAT EXACT MOMENT, BOB WOODWARD KNEW
THAT THIS WAS NOT THE "DEEP THROAT"
HE WAS THERE TO MEET.

MIKE GRASTON
Courtesy Windsor Star

JIM LANGE
Courtesy Daily Oklahoman

STEVE BREEN
Courtesy San Diego Union-Tribune

JOHN BRANCH
Courtesy San Antonio Express-News

GARY VARVEL
Courtesy Indianapolis Star

BRUCE PLANTE
Courtesy Chattanooga Times

JIM HOPE
Courtesy Culpepper News (Va.)

WITH HIS "NOT GUILTY" VERDICT JUST DAYS OLD,
THE SELF PROCLAIMED KING of POP WAS SEEN AT A
WAL-MART TODAY. IT IS SAID THAT JACKSON HEARD
THAT BOY'S PANTS WERE HALF OFF...

JOSEPH F. O'MAHONEY
Courtesy The Patriot Ledger (Mass.)

DANI AGUILA
Courtesy Filipino Reporter

WALT HANDELSMAN
Courtesy Newsday

GENE HERNDON
Courtesy Noblesville Daily Times (Ind.)

85

WAYNE STAYSKAL
Courtesy Tribune Media Services

KARL WIMER
Courtesy Denver Business Journal

Congress

Despite the need for increased spending to rebuild the hurricane-ravaged Gulf Coast, Congress continued to promote a wide variety of "pork" projects. One of the most notorious was Alaska's "Bridge to Nowhere," a $223-million boondoggle to connect Ketchikan, Alaska (population 14,500), to Gravina Island (population 50).

As Senate Democrats continued to delay a vote on judicial nominations by President Bush, Republicans threatened to change the rules. The Democrats referred to the possible rule change as "the nuclear option," but the opposition contended that the nominees had the right to an up or down vote. A bipartisan group hammered out what appeared to be an acceptable compromise that would preserve the right to filibuster in certain cases.

House Majority Leader Tom DeLay was indicted on charges of money laundering in the handling of campaign funds, and Senate Majority Leader Bill Frist's financial dealings came under scrutiny.

Congress passed a massive package to promote new and cleaner energy sources, and after years of debate, the Senate approved drilling for oil in Alaska's Arctic National Wildlife Refuge. A huge new drug benefit program, Medicare Part D, was launched on January 1, 2006.

GARY MARKSTEIN
Courtesy Copley News Service

PAUL COMBS
Courtesy Tampa Tribune

"WELL, THERE GOES THE NEIGHBORHOOD"

DANIEL FENECH
Courtesy Saline Reporter

PETER DUNLAP-SHOHL
Courtesy Anchorage Daily News

ANY PORK IN A STORM.

88

TOM BECK
Courtesy Freeport Journal-Standard (Ill.)

BEN SARGENT
Courtesy Austin American-Statesman

MARK STREETER
Courtesy Savannah Morning News

REX BABIN
Courtesy Sacramento Bee

PETER DUNLAP-SHOHL
Courtesy Anchorage Daily News

ED GAMBLE
Courtesy Florida Times-Union

ROGER SCHILLERSTROM
Courtesy Crain Communications

STEPHEN TEMPLETON
Courtesy The Observer-Times (Pa.)

JERRY HOLBERT
Courtesy Boston Herald

JIM BORGMAN
Courtesy Cincinnati Enquirer

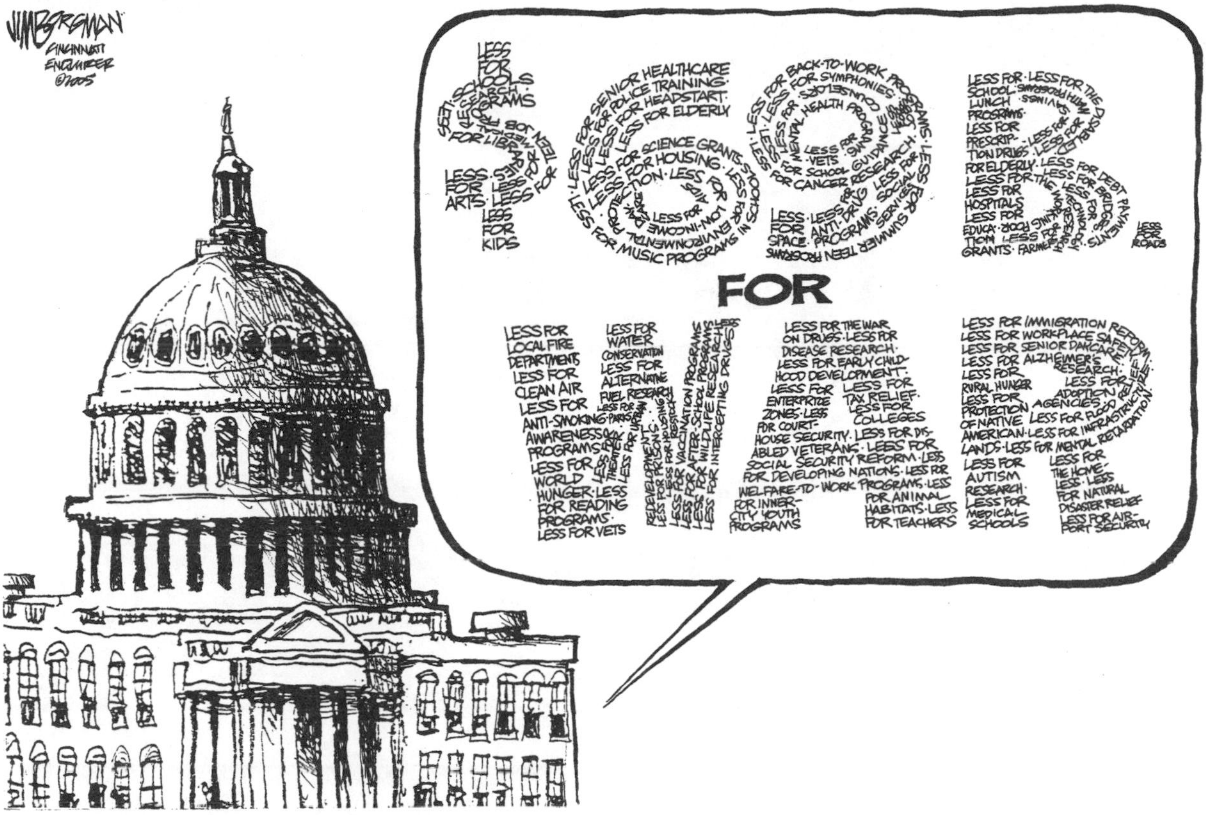
$69B.
FOR
WAR

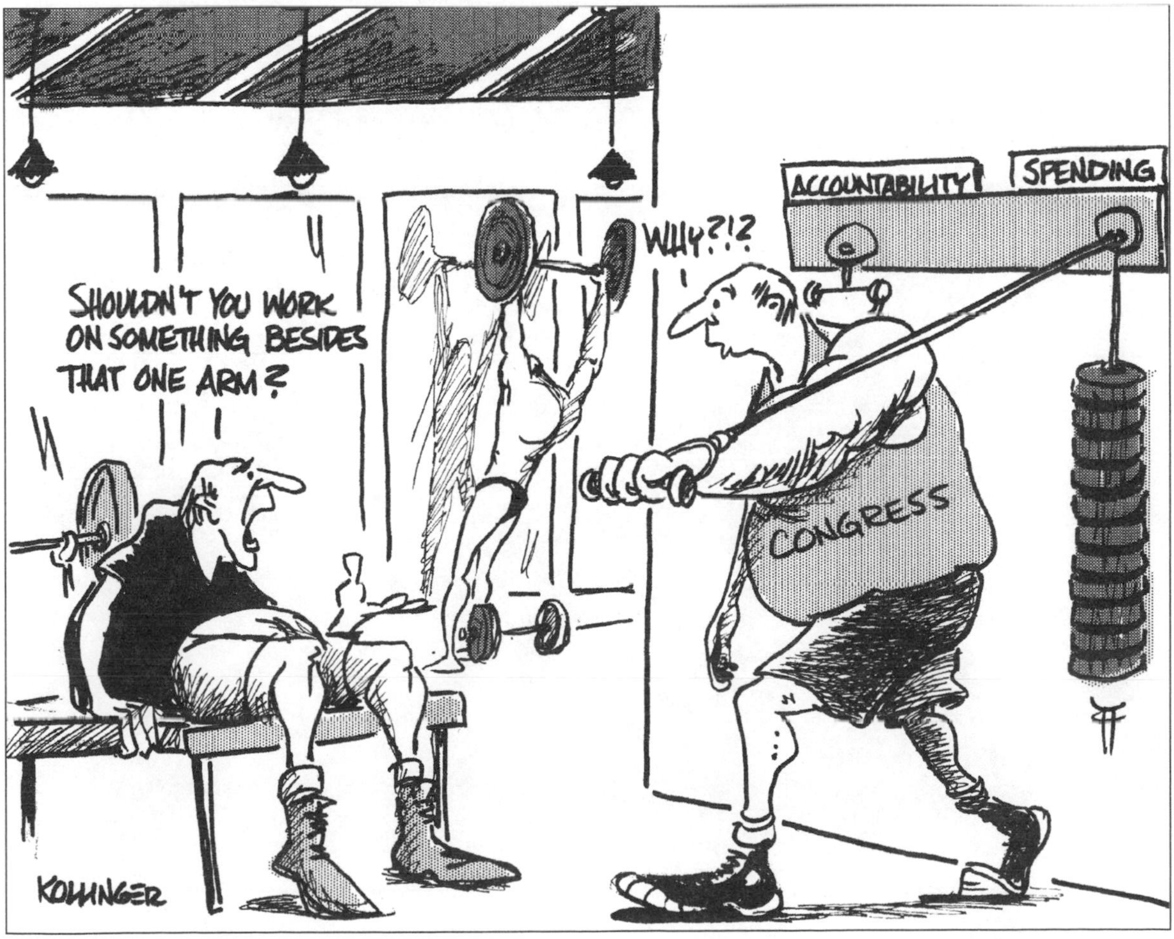
ACCOUNTABILITY
SPENDING
WHY?!?
SHOULDN'T YOU WORK ON SOMETHING BESIDES THAT ONE ARM?
CONGRESS
KOLLINGER

RICK KOLLINGER
Courtesy The Star-Democrat (Md.)

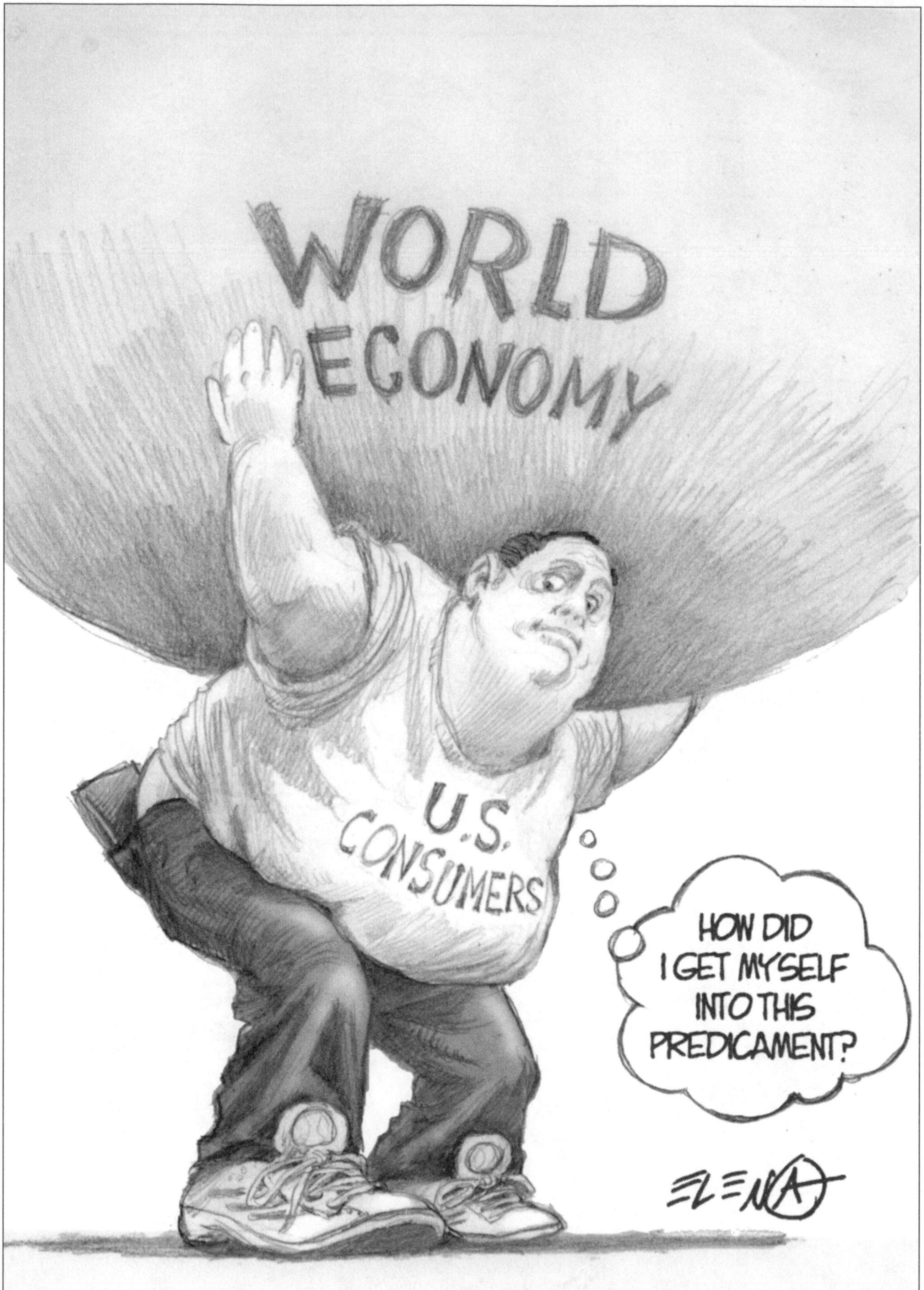
WORLD ECONOMY
U.S. CONSUMERS
HOW DID I GET MYSELF INTO THIS PREDICAMENT?
ELENA

ELENA STEIER
Courtesy The Valley News

The Economy

Despite being walloped by hurricanes, the nation's economy showed steady growth, creating more than 2 million jobs during the year. The stock market remained high, with the Dow Jones hovering around 10,500. There were fears that home heating-fuel prices would sky-rocket because of the damage inflicted on the oil industry in the gulf. That in turn prompted fears that consumers might then cut back on purchases.

The U.S. dependence on foreign oil remains a serious problem and contributes to soaring gas prices. A major aspect of the problem has been the lack of growth in America's refining capacity. The nation's current refining capability of 16.9 million barrels a day, while up from the mid-1990s, remains below the 1981 peak. In addition, emerging Third World markets in China and India are consuming much more oil, further increasing worldwide demand.

In the housing industry, there is concern that rapid increases in home prices, sustained for several years by low mortgage rates, have created dangerous bubbles in some markets.

Longtime Federal Reserve Chairman Alan Greenspan announced his retirement, and President Bush named Ben Bernanke, known as a cautious inflation fighter, to succeed him.

MIKE PETERS
Courtesy Dayton Daily News

95

ETTA HULME
Courtesy Ft. Worth Star-Telegram

JERRY BARNETT
Courtesy Boonville Standard (Ind.)

JIM BUSH
Courtesy Providence Journal (R.I.)

JUSTIN DeFREITAS
Courtesy Berkeley Daily Planet

GASOLINE DELIVERY, 2006

KARL WIMER
Courtesy Denver Business Journal

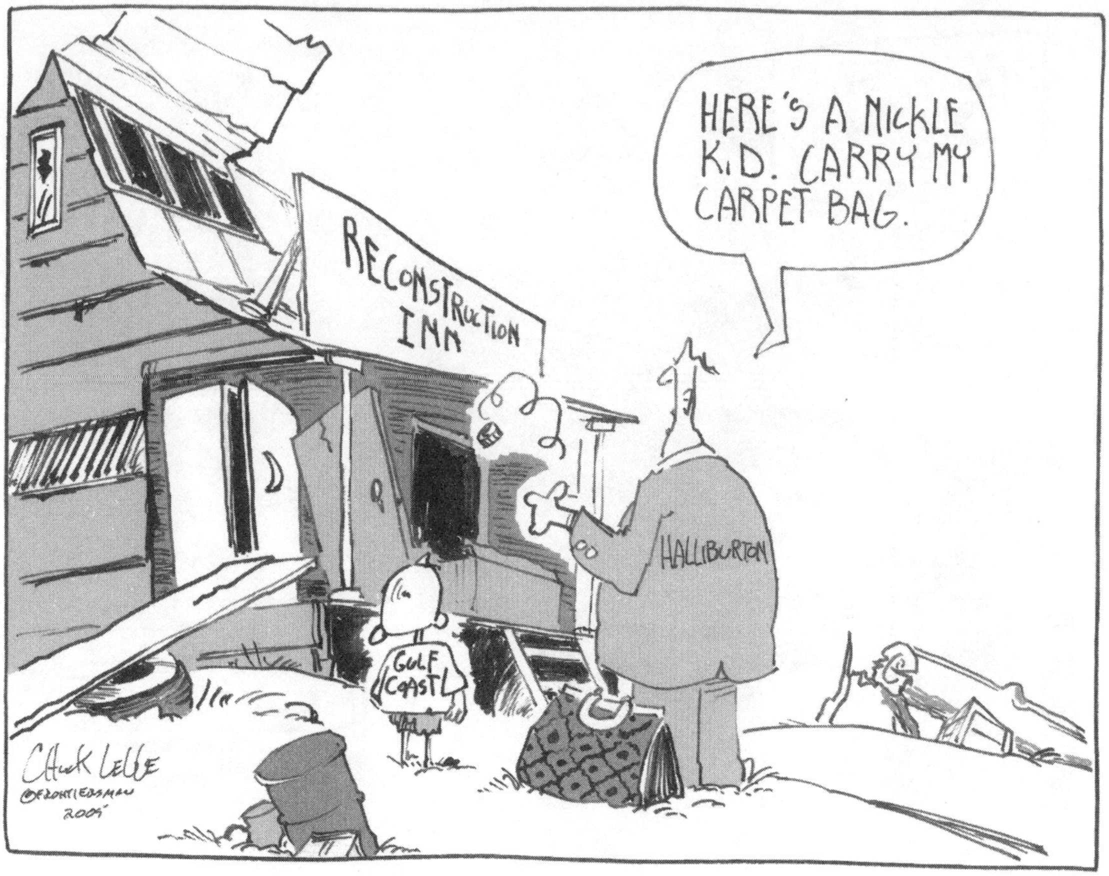
HERE'S A NICKLE K.D. CARRY MY CARPET BAG.
RECONSTRUCTION INN
HALLIBURTON
GULF COAST
CHUCK LEGGE
©FRONTIERSMAN 2005

CHUCK LEGGE
Courtesy The Frontiersman

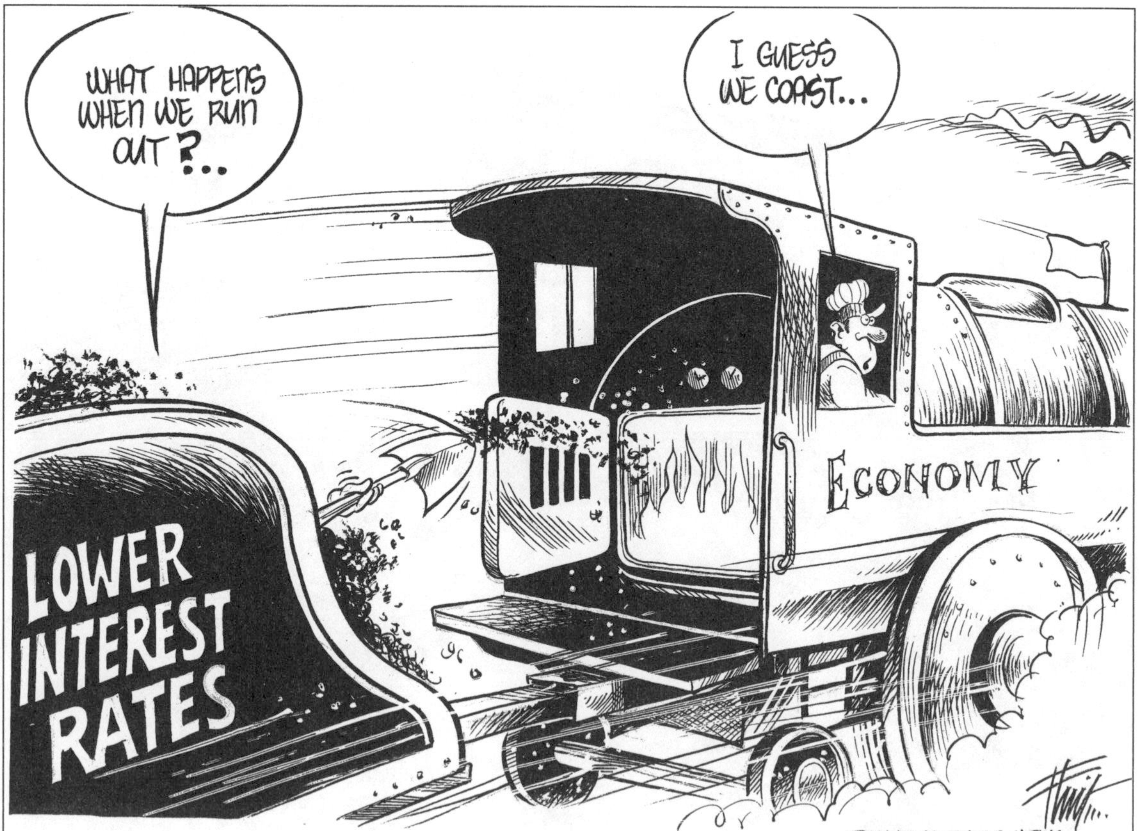
WHAT HAPPENS WHEN WE RUN OUT?..
I GUESS WE COAST...
ECONOMY
LOWER INTEREST RATES
DALLAS MORNING NEWS

WILLIAM FLINT
Courtesy Dallas Morning News

MARSHALL TOOMEY
Courtesy Santa Clarita Signal

ROSS GOSSE
Courtesy Pine Tree Syndicate

STEVE YORK
Courtesy Kankakee Daily Journal

WILLIAM FLINT
Courtesy Dallas Morning News

PATRICK O'CONNOR
Courtesy Los Angeles Daily News

KEVIN KALLAUGHER
Courtesy Baltimore Sun

KARL WIMER
Courtesy Denver Business Journal

DANIEL FENECH
Courtesy Saline Reporter

BILL SMITH
Courtesy Lompoc Record (Calif.)

BRUCE PLANTE
Courtesy Chattanooga Times

BRUCE QUAST
Courtesy Rockford Register-Star

STEVE KELLEY
Courtesy The Times-Picayune (La.)

STEVE BREEN
Courtesy San Diego Union-Tribune

PATRICK O'CONNOR
Courtesy Los Angeles Daily News

JOHN DEERING
Courtesy Arkansas Democrat-Gazette

JEFF PARKER
Courtesy Florida Today

105

AARON TAYLOR
Courtesy Provo Daily Herald

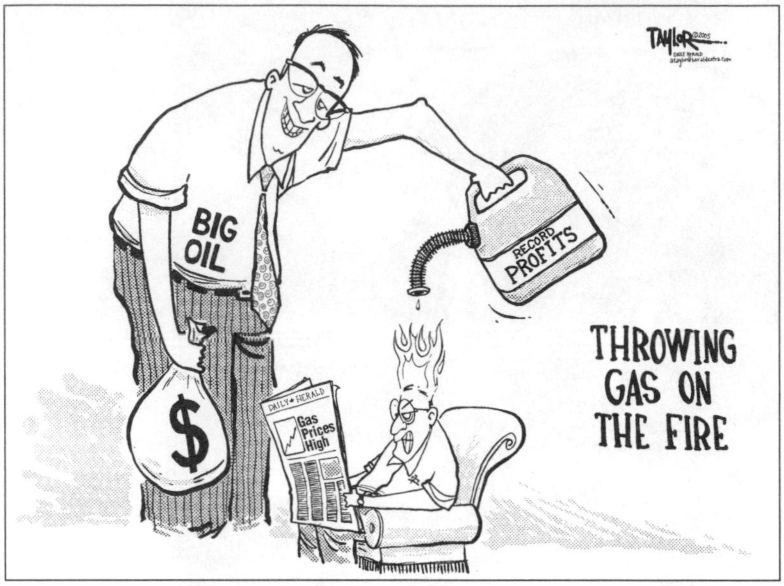
BIG OIL
RECORD PROFITS
DAILY HERALD
Gas Prices High
THROWING GAS ON THE FIRE

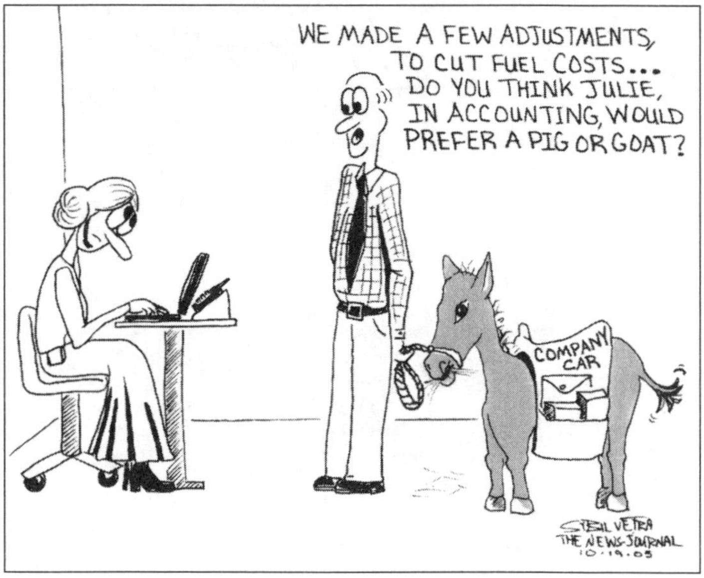
WE MADE A FEW ADJUSTMENTS, TO CUT FUEL COSTS... DO YOU THINK JULIE, IN ACCOUNTING, WOULD PREFER A PIG OR GOAT?
COMPANY CAR
SYBIL VETRA THE NEWS-JOURNAL 10-19-05

SYBIL VETRA
Courtesy The News-Journal (N.C.)

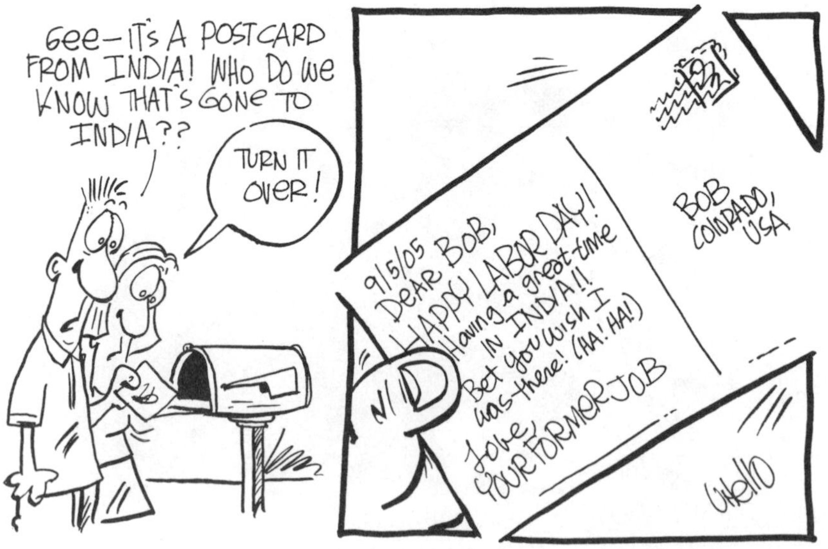
GEE—IT'S A POSTCARD FROM INDIA! WHO DO WE KNOW THAT'S GONE TO INDIA??
TURN IT OVER!
9/5/05 DEAR BOB, HAPPY LABOR DAY! Having a great time IN INDIA!! Bet you wish I was there! (HA! HA!) Love, YOUR FORMER JOB
BOB COLORADO, USA
Vitello

ALAN VITELLO
Courtesy Greeley Tribune

ROB HARRIMAN
Courtesy Portland Tribune

ALAN NASH
Courtesy Gering Courier/North Platte Bulletin

JEFF STAHLER
Courtesy Columbus Dispatch

FRED CURATOLO
Courtesy Edmonton Journal

FRANK PAGE
Courtesy Rome Daily Sentinel (N.Y.)

JAMES CASCIARI
Courtesy Treasure Coast Newspapers

WALT HANDELSMAN
Courtesy Newsday

S. C. RAWLS
Courtesy Rockdale Citizen

JOE HOFFECKER
Courtesy American City Business Journals

BOB UNELL
Courtesy Kansas City Star

TERRY WISE
Courtesy Ratland Ink Press

DOUG MacGREGOR
Courtesy Ft. Myers News-Press

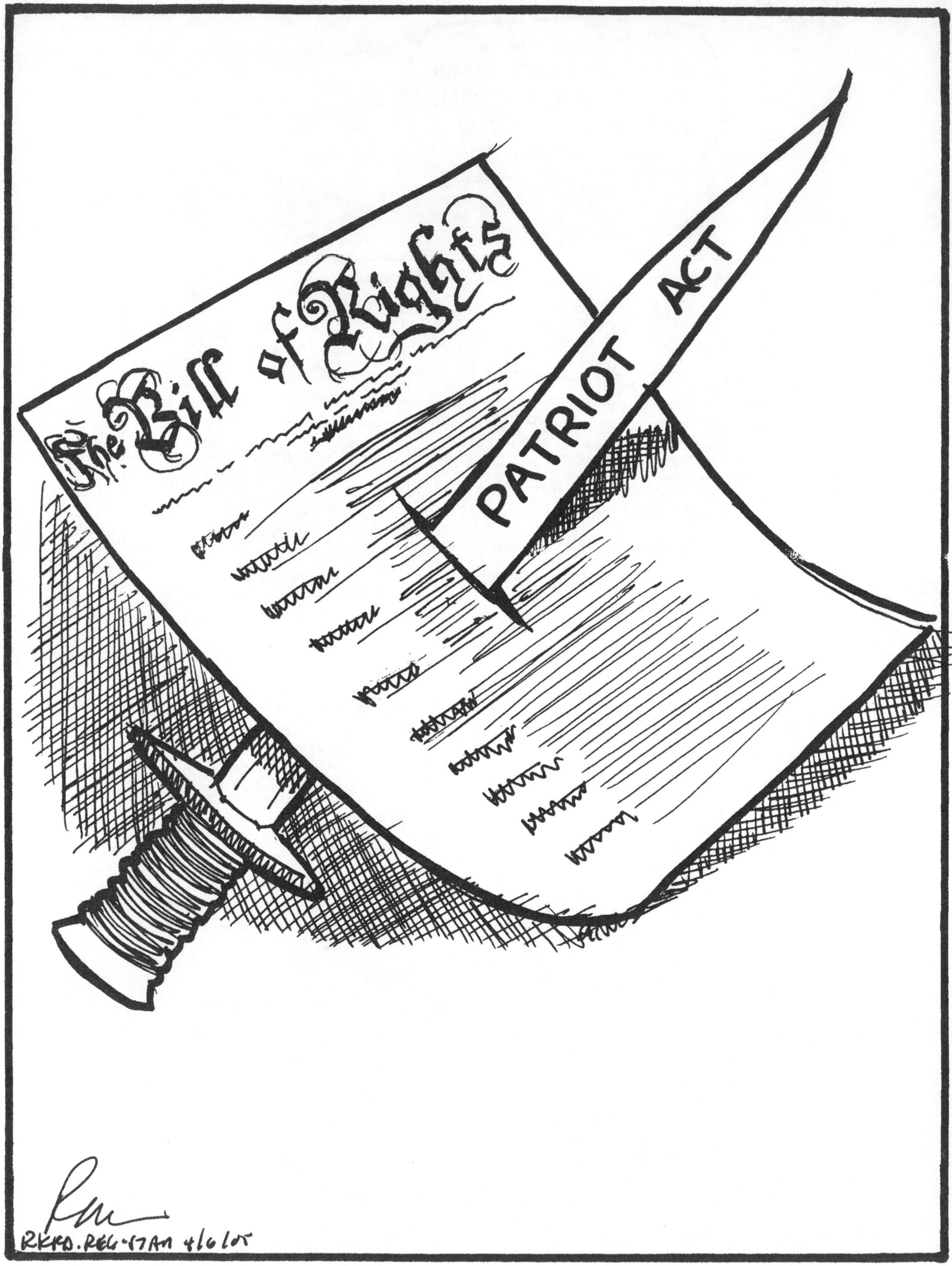
The Bill of Rights
PATRIOT ACT
RKFD. REG-STAR 4/6/05

BOB WIEGERS
Courtesy Rockford Register-Star

Government

A rising tide of problems confronted the Republican Party during the year: the indictment of House leader Tom DeLay, a federal investigation into Sen. Bill Frist's finances, and the indictment of Scooter Libby. But another potential catastrophe for the party loomed larger and larger: absolute, unrestrained, runaway spending.

Historically the party of fiscal responsibility and small government, the GOP threatened to give new meaning to the concept of spend . . . and spend . . . and spend. Even the optimists say the deficit for the current fiscal year will reach $455 billion. Discretionary spending—outlays above and beyond expenditures for defense—soared by 21 percent during the first three years of the Bush Administration. Costly programs included the homeland security bill and the farm bill. And the gigantic prescription-drug entitlement program promises to force the budget even further into the red.

As if that weren't enough, the Bush Administration did little in 2005 to stem the flow of illegal immigration. Nearly eleven million undocumented immigrants now reside in the United States, and some 800,000 more arrive each year.

Bankruptcy filings surged in October as many cash-strapped citizens raced to beat a change in the law making it harder for consumers to wipe out big debts.

NICK ANDERSON
Courtesy Louisville Courier-Journal

PAUL COMBS
Courtesy Tampa Tribune

JOHN AUCTER
Courtesy Grand Rapids Business Journal

SCOTT STANTIS
Courtesy Birmingham News

PAUL FELL
Courtesy Lincoln Journal Star

BRIAN DUFFY
Courtesy Des Moines Register

DAVID COX
Courtesy Arkansas Democrat-Gazette

STEVE BREEN
Courtesy San Diego Union-Tribune

BILL MANGOLD
Courtesy Heritage Newspapers

JOE R. LANE
Courtesy Denton Record-Chronicle

JACK HIGGINS
Courtesy Chicago Sun-Times

SCOTT STANTIS
Courtesy Birmingham News

THE GREAT SATAN

PAUL FELL
Courtesy Lincoln Journal Star

DARREL AKERS
Courtesy The Reporter (Calif.)

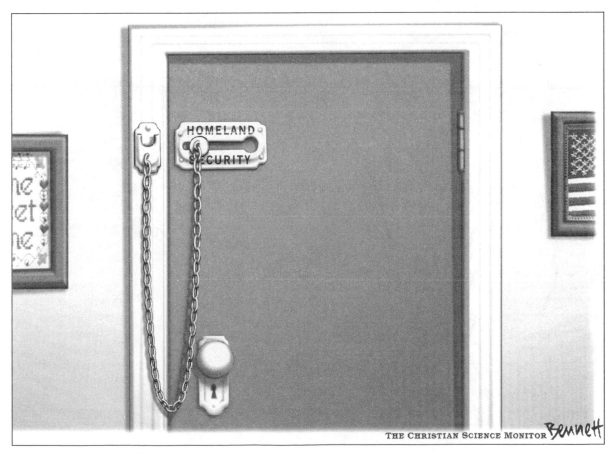

CLAY BENNETT
Courtesy Christian Science Monitor

JERRY GARDEN
Courtesy UTP Voice (Calif.)

Health / Education

The worldwide medical community expressed growing concern about the spread of the H5N1 avian flu virus, which by late 2005 had caused dozens of deaths in Southeast Asia. Health professionals feared the virus might adapt to a form that could be readily transmitted to humans, which could create a global pandemic. Scientists launched a major effort to develop medicines to combat the threat.

The House passed a bill to expand federal funding of embryonic stem cell research, although the Senate continued to ponder the issue. Stem cell research may help find cures for certain diseases, but the process destroys the embryo, which is considered human life by many people. President Bush has promised to veto the bill if it reaches his desk.

Several states have demanded that the concept of "intelligent design," which acknowledges the role of some higher power in the development of life, be taught along with Charles Darwin's Theory of Evolution.

The Pledge of Allegiance was tested in the courts, and educators complained that President Bush's No Child Left Behind program placed too much emphasis on test scores. It was alleged that some school districts were concentrating more on teaching students how to take tests than promoting genuine learning.

J. D. CROWE
Courtesy Mobile Register

JERRY HOLBERT
Courtesy Boston Herald

CHARLIE HALL
Courtesy Rhode Island News Group

SYBIL VETRA
Courtesy The News-Journal (N.C.)

WAYNE STAYSKAL
Courtesy Tribune Media Services

WILLIAM WALLACE
Courtesy Casper Star-Tribune

CHUCK ASAY
Courtesy Colorado Springs Gazette-Telegraph

ANNETTE BALESTERI
Courtesy Ledger Dispatch (Calif.)

JESSE SPRINGER
Courtesy Eugene Register-Guard

124

BOB UNELL
Courtesy Kansas City Star

CLAY BENNETT
Courtesy Christian Science Monitor

JACK CHAPMAN
Courtesy Desoto Times Today

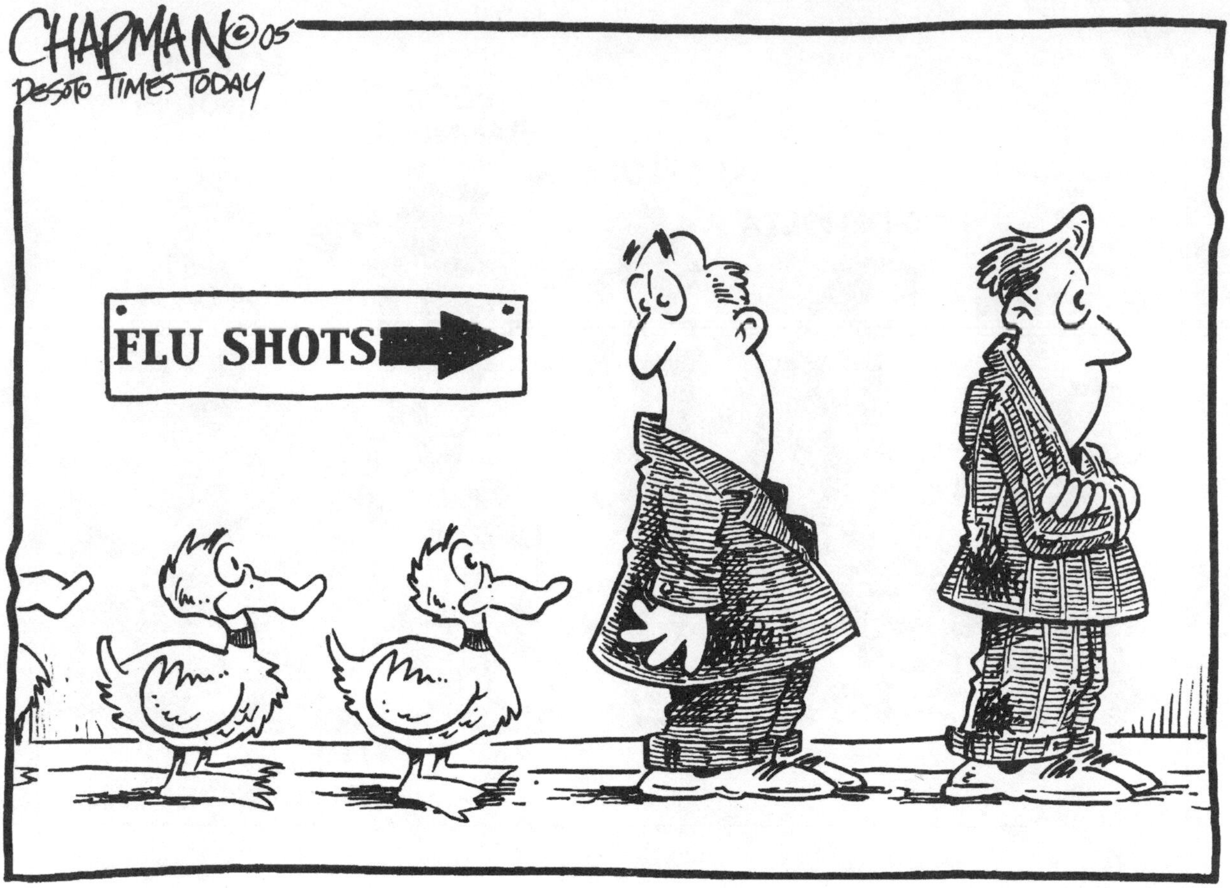
CHAPMAN©05
DESOTO TIMES TODAY
FLU SHOTS

JONATHAN TODD
Courtesy Shreveport Times

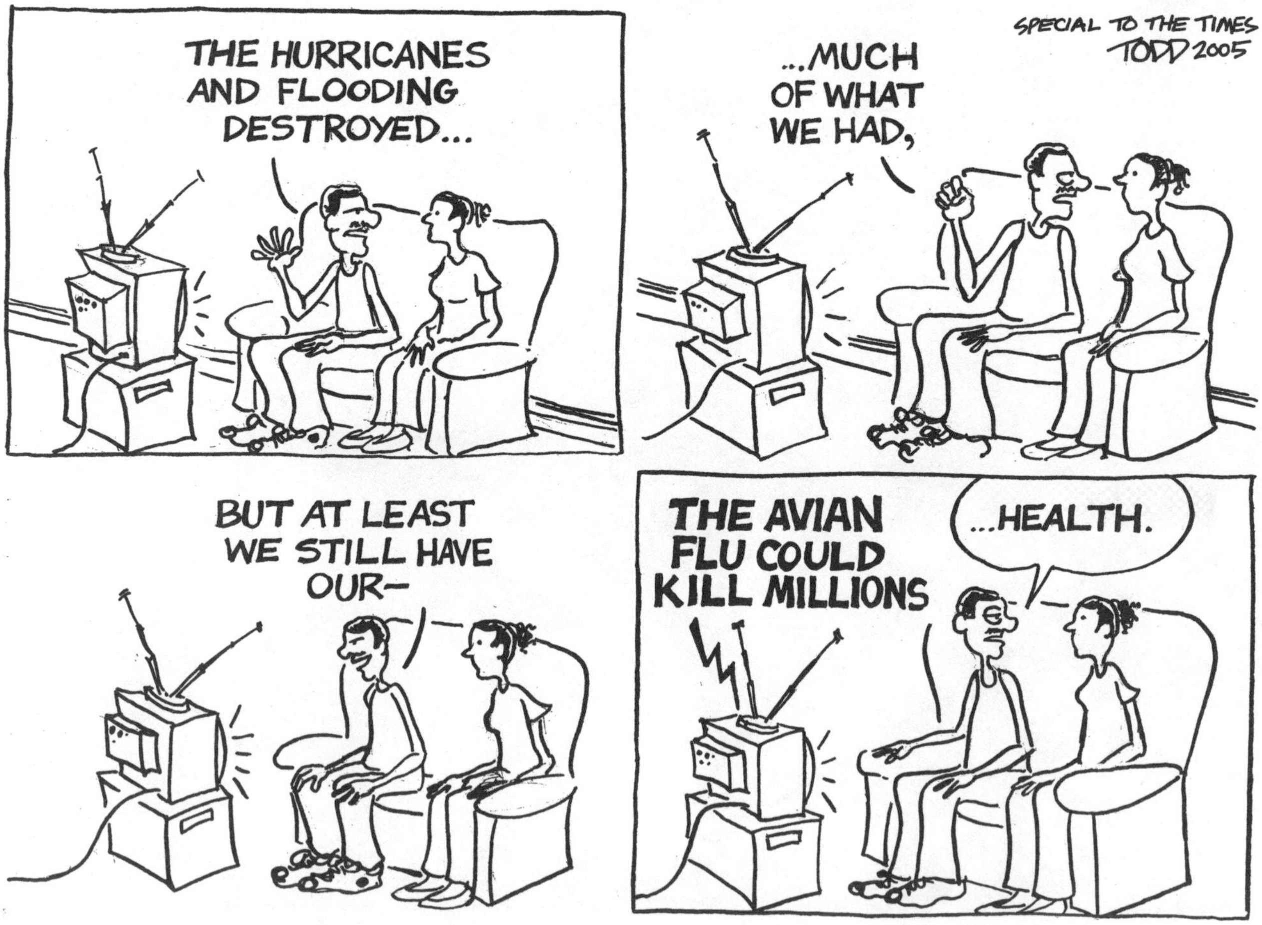
SPECIAL TO THE TIMES
TODD 2005
THE HURRICANES AND FLOODING DESTROYED...
...MUCH OF WHAT WE HAD,
BUT AT LEAST WE STILL HAVE OUR–
THE AVIAN FLU COULD KILL MILLIONS
...HEALTH.

MICHAEL RAMIREZ
Courtesy Los Angeles Times

THE SCARIEST COSTUME THIS HALLOWEEN

TRICK OR TREAT

BILL JANOCHA
Courtesy Stamford Times

JEFF STAHLER
Courtesy Columbus Dispatch

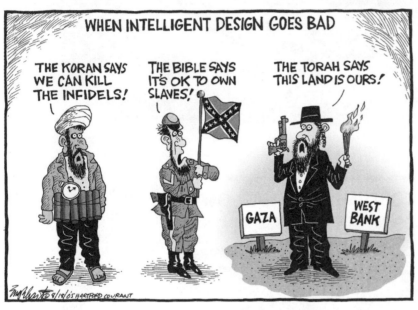

BOB ENGLEHART
Courtesy Hartford Courant

JON RICHARDS
Courtesy Albuquerque Journal North

AARON TAYLOR
Courtesy Provo Daily Herald

JOHN SHERFFIUS
Courtesy jsherffius@aol.com

The coming pandemic

MIKE LESTER
Courtesy Rome News-Tribune (Ga.)

MIKE KEEFE
Courtesy Denver Post

MIKE LUCKOVICH
Courtesy Atlanta Journal-Constitution

ED COLLEY
Courtesy Boston Globe South

Area towns are looking for alternate ways to trim health care costs.

STEVE SACK
Courtesy Minneapolis Star-Tribune

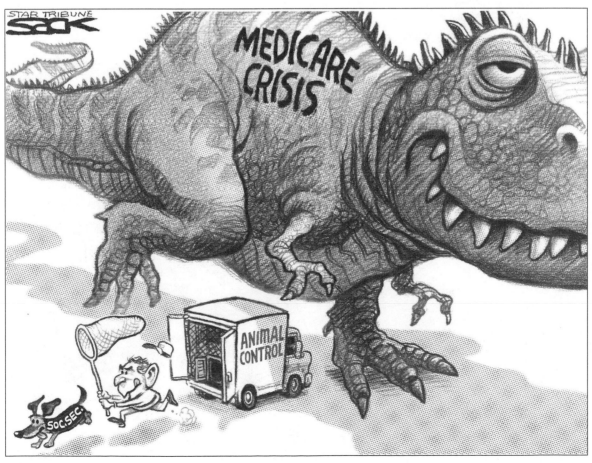

RICHARD WALLMEYER
Courtesy Long Beach Press-Telegram

BOB ENGLEHART
Courtesy Hartford Courant

"SO FAR, ALL WE'RE LEARNING IS HOW TO TAKE A MATH TEST, HOW TO TAKE A SCIENCE TEST, AND HOW TO TAKE A READING TEST."

ANNETTE BALESTERI
Courtesy Ledger Dispatch (Calif.)

BILL MANGOLD
Courtesy Heritage Newspapers

MIKE KEEFE
Courtesy Denver Post

ROGER HARVELL
Courtesy Greenville News-Piedmont

BRUCE BEATTIE
Courtesy Daytona Beach News-Journal

"Oh, look . . . they're reading '1984' in Ms. Smith's English class."

WAYNE STROOT
Courtesy Hastings Tribune

BRIAN DUFFY
Courtesy Des Moines Register

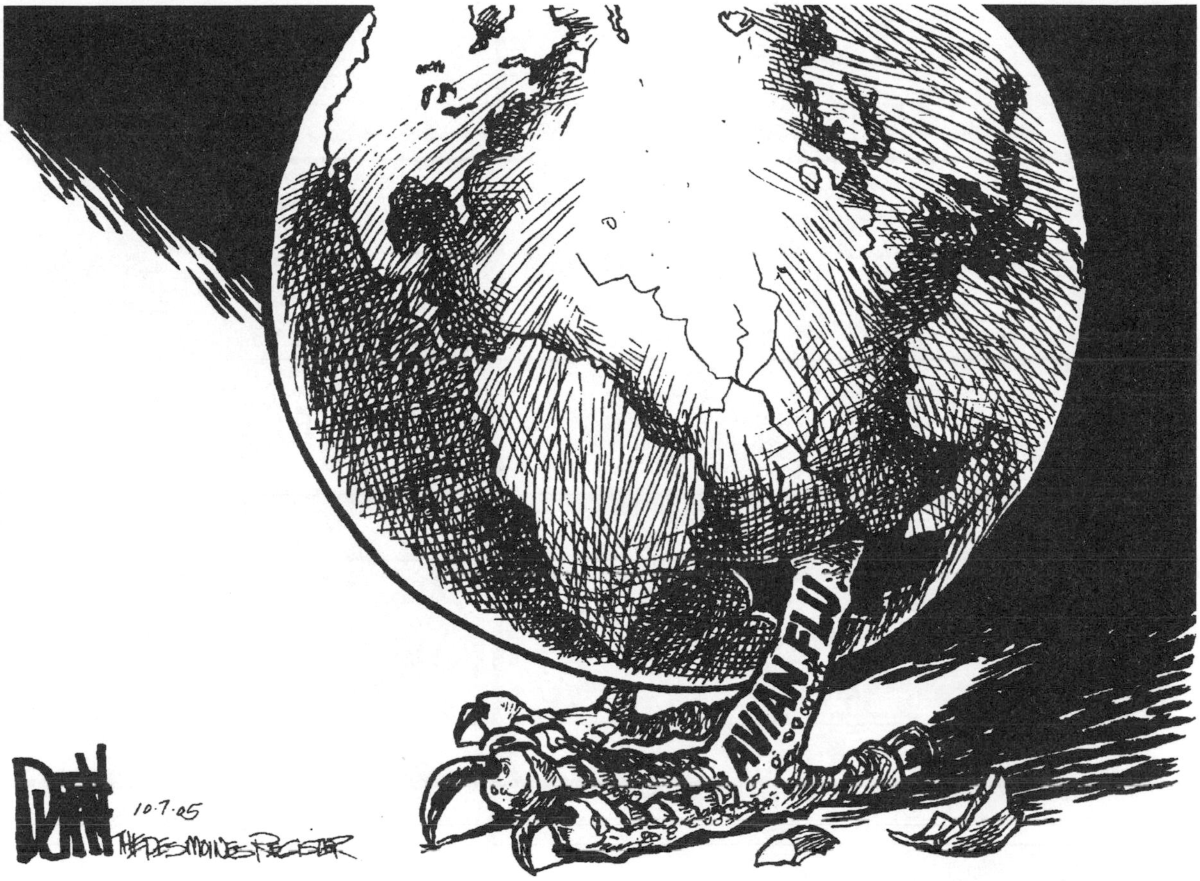
AVIAN FLU
10·7·05
THE DES MOINES REGISTER

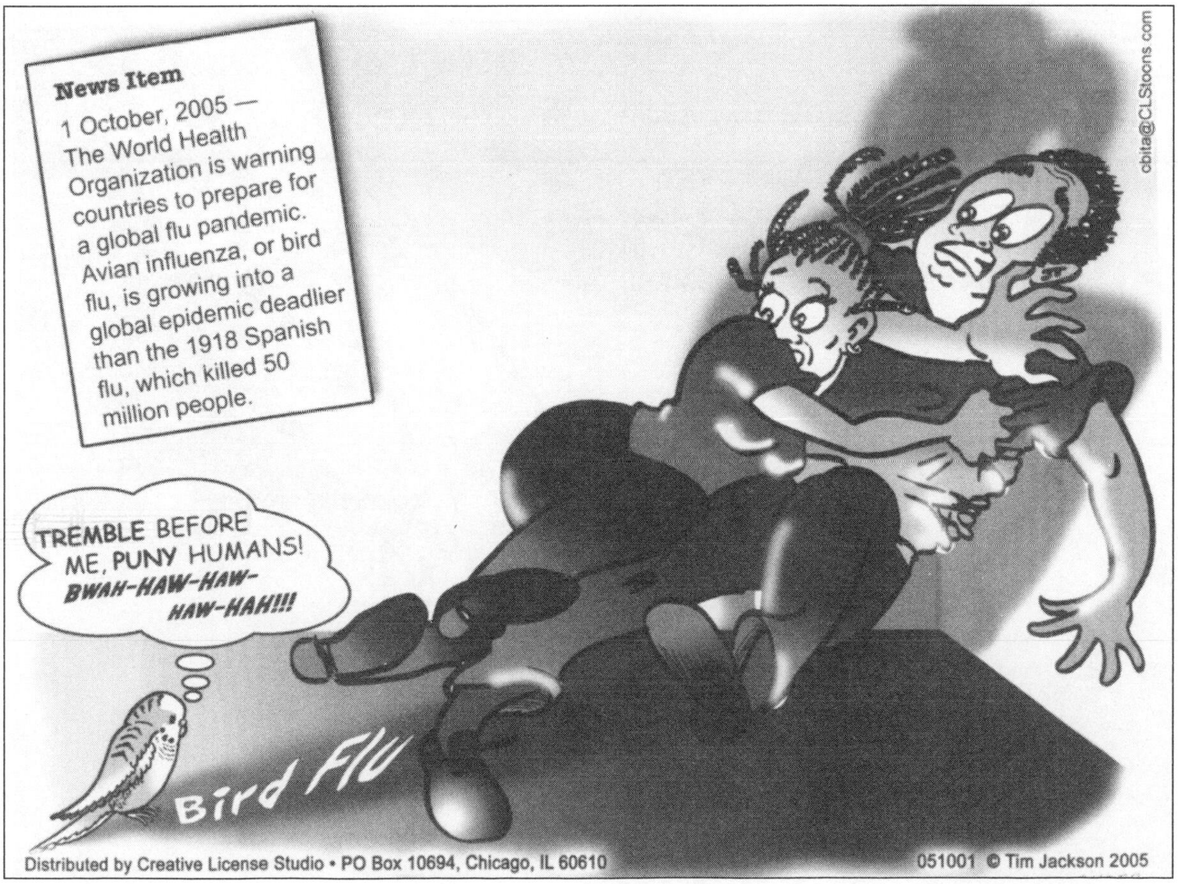
News Item
1 October, 2005 — The World Health Organization is warning countries to prepare for a global flu pandemic. Avian influenza, or bird flu, is growing into a global epidemic deadlier than the 1918 Spanish flu, which killed 50 million people.
TREMBLE BEFORE ME, PUNY HUMANS! BWAH-HAW-HAW-HAW-HAH!!!
Bird FLU
cbita@CLStoons.com
Distributed by Creative License Studio • PO Box 10694, Chicago, IL 60610
051001 © Tim Jackson 2005

TIM JACKSON
Courtesy Chicago Defender

STEVE GREENBERG
Courtesy Ventura County Star

FRANK PAGE
Courtesy Rome Daily Sentinel (N.Y.)

Sports

After an 88-year drought, the Chicago White Sox won the National League pennant, ending the so-called "Black Sox" curse of 1917, just as the Boston Red Sox broke the "Babe Ruth" curse in 2004. The White Sox went on to beat the Houston Astros in the World Series in four straight games.

Allegations of steroid use by professional athletes continued to plague sports. Former major league baseball star Jose Canseco's book *Juiced* described rampant use of the illegal drug in team clubhouses. Suspicion fell on a lengthy list of players. Congress held hearings, and the House Government Reform Committee scolded professional baseball for its failure to deal with the problem.

President Bush called on players, owners, and coaches to get tough on steroids for the sake of young people who see drugs as the only way to compete at the highest levels. According to a study by the Centers for Disease Control and Prevention, more than half a million teenagers have tried steroids, triple the number of a decade ago.

A player strike that threatened the National Hockey League season was resolved, but teams in Atlanta, Nashville, Phoenix, Washington, and Carolina continued to suffer from declining attendance.

KEVIN KALLAUGHER
Courtesy Baltimore Sun

137

MIKE SCOTT
Courtesy Newark Star-Ledger

CHARLIE HALL
Courtesy Rhode Island News Group

DON LANDGREN JR.
Courtesy The Landmark

POL GALVEZ
Courtesy Philippine News

ROSS GOSSE
Courtesy Pine Tree Syndicate

CLAY BENNETT
Courtesy Christian Science Monitor

JOE MAJESKI
Courtesy Wilkes-Barre Times-Leader

JIMMY MARGULIES
Courtesy The Record (N.J.)

"I take it, Mr. Commissioner, nodding your head means you agree baseball is dealing effectively with steroid abuse?"

STEVE KELLEY
Courtesy The Times-Picayune (La.)

CHRIS BRITT
Courtesy State Journal-Register (Ill.)

WILL O'TOOLE
Courtesy Home News & Tribune

MIKE GRASTON
Courtesy Windsor Sta

NEIL GRAHAME
Courtesy Spencer Newspapers

JACK HIGGINS
Courtesy Chicago Sun-Times

(Chicago White Sox finally win World Series)

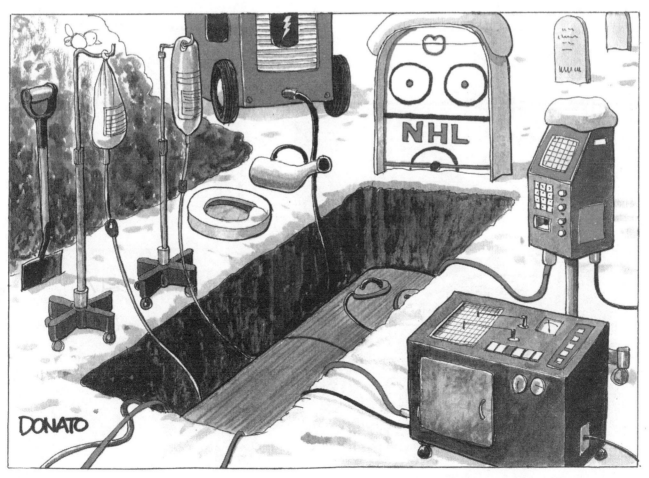

ANDY DONATO
Courtesy Toronto Sun

THEO MOUDAKIS
Courtesy Toronto Star

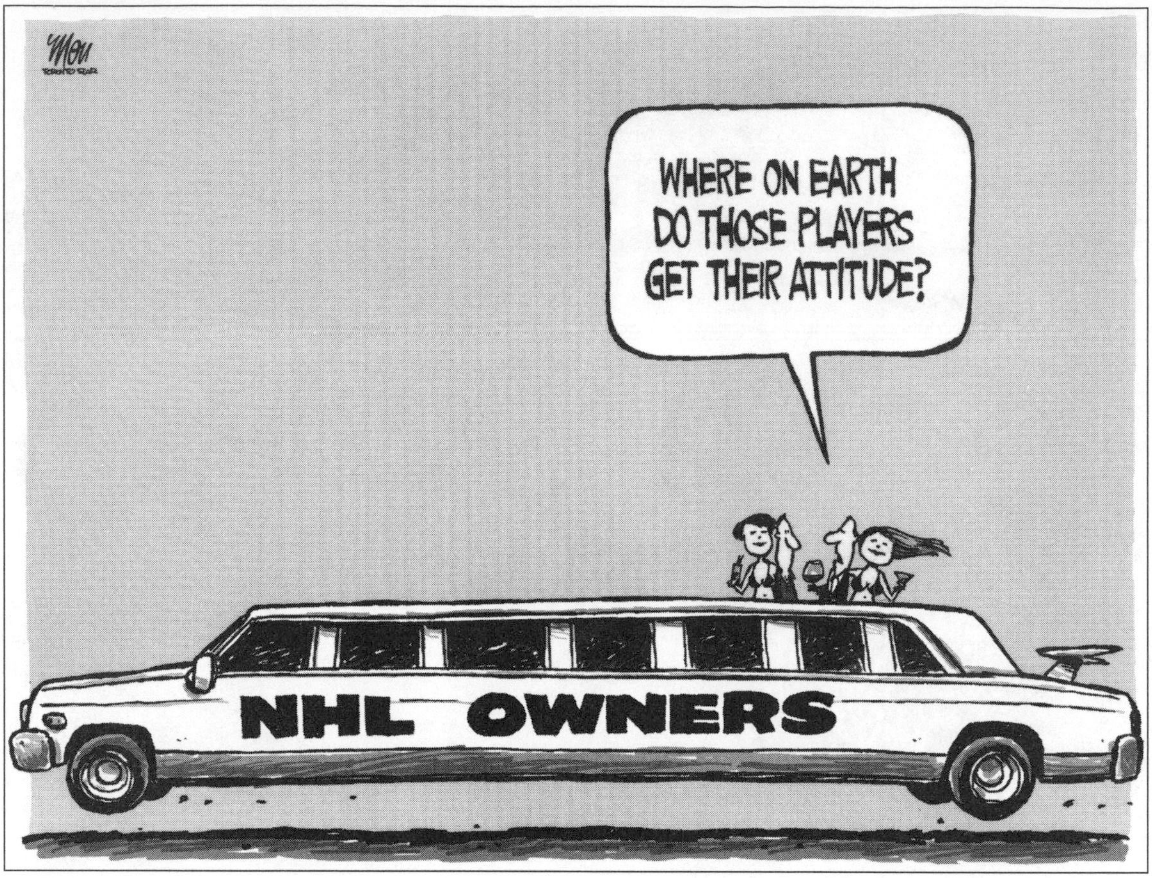
WHERE ON EARTH DO THOSE PLAYERS GET THEIR ATTITUDE?
NHL OWNERS

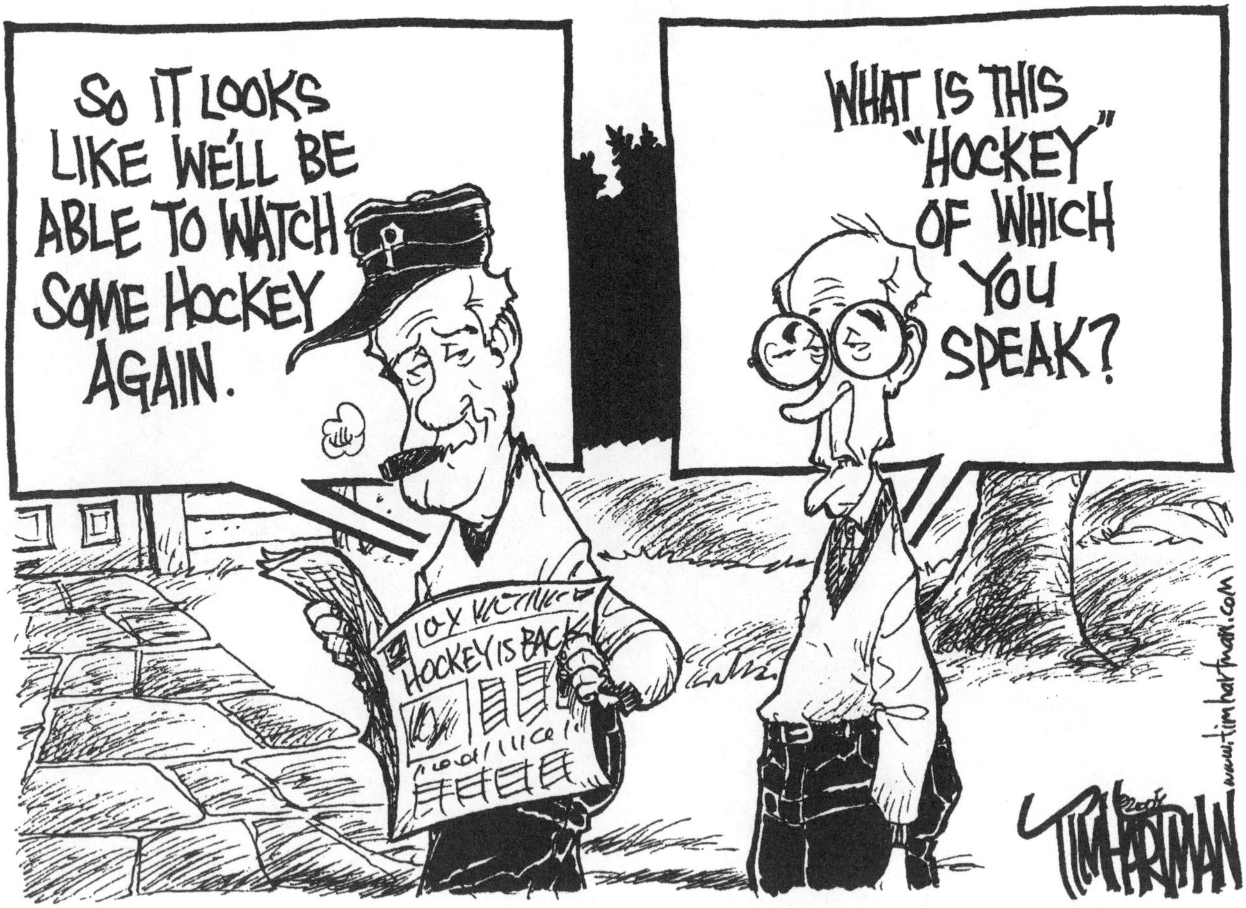
SO IT LOOKS LIKE WE'LL BE ABLE TO WATCH SOME HOCKEY AGAIN.
WHAT IS THIS "HOCKEY" OF WHICH YOU SPEAK?
HOCKEY IS BACK
www.timhartman.com
TIM HARTMAN

TIM HARTMAN
Courtesy Beaver County Times-Record (Pa.)

Space / Air Travel

NASA cancelled scheduled space shuttle flights after a piece of foam insulation broke off of an external fuel tank during the launch of Discovery. As the astronauts continued their mission to the international space station, delivering long-awaited supplies and replacement parts, engineers on Earth analyzed photographs to determine if the shuttle's fragile protective tiles had sustained damage that could jeopardize the return flight.

For the first time, astronauts visited the underside of a space shuttle in flight. They removed two protruding gap-fillers in the tiles, and the shuttle completed its mission and returned to Earth safely on schedule.

Two astronauts on China's second manned space flight landed to a heroes' welcome. Beijing called the five-day mission a triumph for the ruling Communist Party and announced its next goal: a space walk in 2007. Voyager probes during the year became the first man-made objects to leave the solar system.

Airlines felt an economic pinch as fuel costs skyrocketed and business nose-dived. Several sought the protection of bankruptcy in order to stay aloft. Competition among the major carriers remained fierce, prompting a wide range of cost-cutting measures, including the elimination of free in-flight meals.

JOHN BRANCH
Courtesy San Antonio Express-News

145

ROGER HARVELL
Courtesy Greenville News-Piedmont

JACK CHAPMAN
Courtesy Desoto Times Today

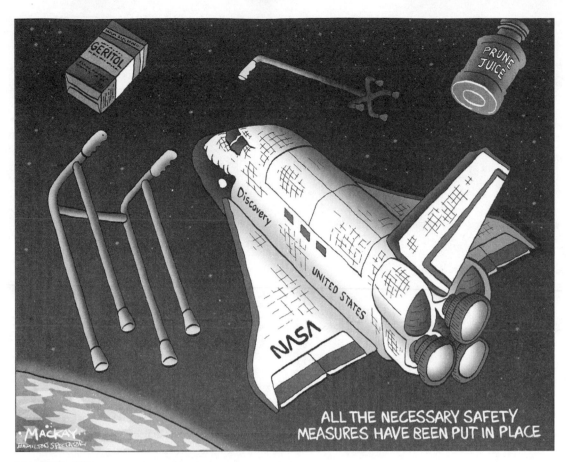

GRAEME MacKAY
Courtesy Hamilton Spectator (Can.)

GARY VARVEL
Courtesy Indianapolis Star

MICHAEL OSBUN
Courtesy Citrus County Chronicle (Fla

FISCAL DISASTERS AND THE AIRLINE INDUSTRY

FRED CURATOLO
Courtesy Edmonton Sun

STEVE LINDSTROM
Courtesy Duluth News-Tribune

DAVID BROWN
Courtesy Los Angeles Sentinel

JEFF PARKER
Courtesy Florida Today

GUY BADEAUX
Courtesy Le Droit (Can.)

ROBERT ARIAIL
Courtesy The State (S.C.)

Foreign Affairs

Revelations in the Iraqi oil-for-food scandal rocked the United Nations during 2005. High-level U.N. officials, as well as highly placed politicians in nations such as France, Russia, and Great Britain, appeared to be implicated in a far-reaching program of kickbacks in oil allocations from Saddam Hussein's sanctions-bound regime.

Israel removed Jewish residents from the Gaza Strip in an effort to further the peace process in the Middle East. Residents who refused to leave were forcibly ejected. The assassination of Lebanese businessman Rafik Hariri sparked massive street protests against Syria, whose leaders were implicated in the murder. The largely peaceful uprising led Syria to withdraw its troops from the country it had occupied for fifteen years.

French voters overwhelmingly rejected the European Union constitution, and Germany elected its first female chancellor. In November, France was virtually paralyzed for a time when riots by discontented Muslim residents erupted in cities across the country.

China made it clear during the year that it is well on the road to becoming an economic and military superpower. Its economy, which is growing at 9 percent a year, will be the second largest in the world by 2020. China is now the world's second-largest consumer of oil.

STEVE McBRIDE
Courtesy Independence Daily Reporter (Kan.)

PAUL NOWAK
Courtesy CNS News.com

MICHAEL THOMPSON
Detroit Free Press

BOB GORRELL
Courtesy Creators Syndicate

THEO MOUDAKIS
Courtesy Toronto Star

ROY PETERSON
Courtesy Vancouver Sun

GEORGE DANBY
Courtesy Bangor Daily News

THEO MOUDAKIS
Courtesy Toronto Star

GRAEME MacKAY
Courtesy Hamilton Spectator (Can.)

DANA SUMMERS
Courtesy Orlando Sentinel

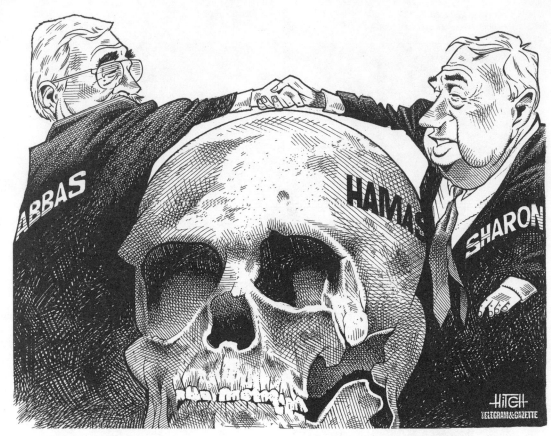

DAVID HITCH
Courtesy Worcester Telegram & Gazette

GARY MARKSTEIN
Courtesy Copley News Service

CLAY BENNETT
Courtesy Christian Science Monitor

JIMMY MARGULIES
Courtesy The Record (N.J.)

WEB OF DECEIT AND DECEPTION

FOOD FOR OIL PROGRAM

UN

OH, WHAT A TANGLED WEB OF MISDEED INDEED!

NY CITY FILIPINO REPORTER

8/19

DANI AGUILA
Courtesy Filipino Reporter

DAVID COX
Courtesy Arkansas Democrat-Gazette

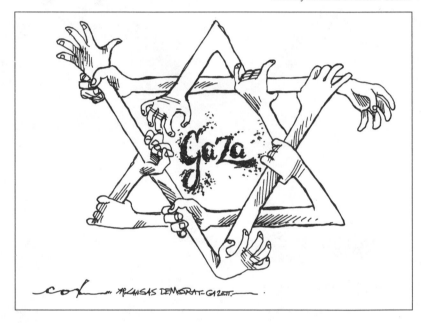

Gaza

ARKANSAS DEMOCRAT-GAZETTE

THE WHITE HOUSE LAUNCHES A P.R. CAMPAIGN TO IMPROVE AMERICA'S IMAGE IN THE ARAB WORLD...

2005
LOWE
TRIBUNE MEDIA
SOUTH FLA. SUN-SENTINEL

CHAN LOWE
Courtesy Fort Lauderdale News/
South Florida Sun-Sentinel

MARSHALL RAMSEY
Courtesy The Clarion-Ledger (Miss.)

STEVE McBRIDE
Courtesy Independence Daily Reporter (Kan.)

LANDGREN THE LANDMARK 2-31-05

GOP LIVING WILL

I hereby appoint...
☐ The president
☐ Congress
☐ The governor
☐ The courts
☐ Far-right religious fanatics
☐ All of the above

to make healthcare decisions on my behalf.

LIVING WILL

I hereby wish that any life-sustaining treatment be...
☐ continued.
☐ stopped.

I also wish to keep the politicians and other opportunists out of my business.

TERRY SCHIAVO'S LEGACY

Politics

Democratic politicians such as Howard Dean and Ted Kennedy continued their relentless attacks on President Bush, repeatedly branding him a liar for his statements leading up to the Iraq war, belittling his handling of the hurricane recovery effort, and attempting to block his cabinet and judicial nominations. Democrats opposed the Republican agenda for tax reform, school choice, and free trade but offered few ideas of their own.

In November, California Gov. Arnold Schwarzenegger suffered a stinging rebuke from voters who rejected all four of his proposals to reshape state government. One of the initiatives voted down would have required that parents be notified when minors seek abortions.

In the final analysis, the election pitted the increasingly unpopular governor against two of California's most powerful political forces—public employee unions and the Democratic Party. It was a sobering defeat for a man once regarded as one of the most popular politicians in America.

The emotional case of Terri Schiavo became a political issue, with conservatives fighting to keep her feeding tube in and liberals supporting her husband's efforts to have it removed. The liberals prevailed.

JOEL THORNHILL
Courtesy Lawrence County Record

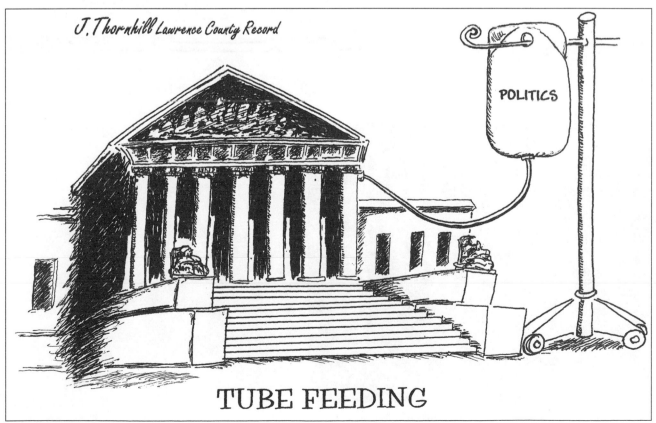

TUBE FEEDING

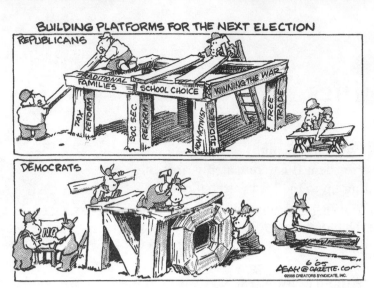

CHUCK ASAY
Courtesy Colorado Springs Gazette-Telegraph

JERRY BARNETT
Courtesy Boonville Standard (Ind.)

DAVID HITCH
Courtesy Worcester Telegram & Gazette

JACK JURDEN
Courtesy Wilmington News-Journal

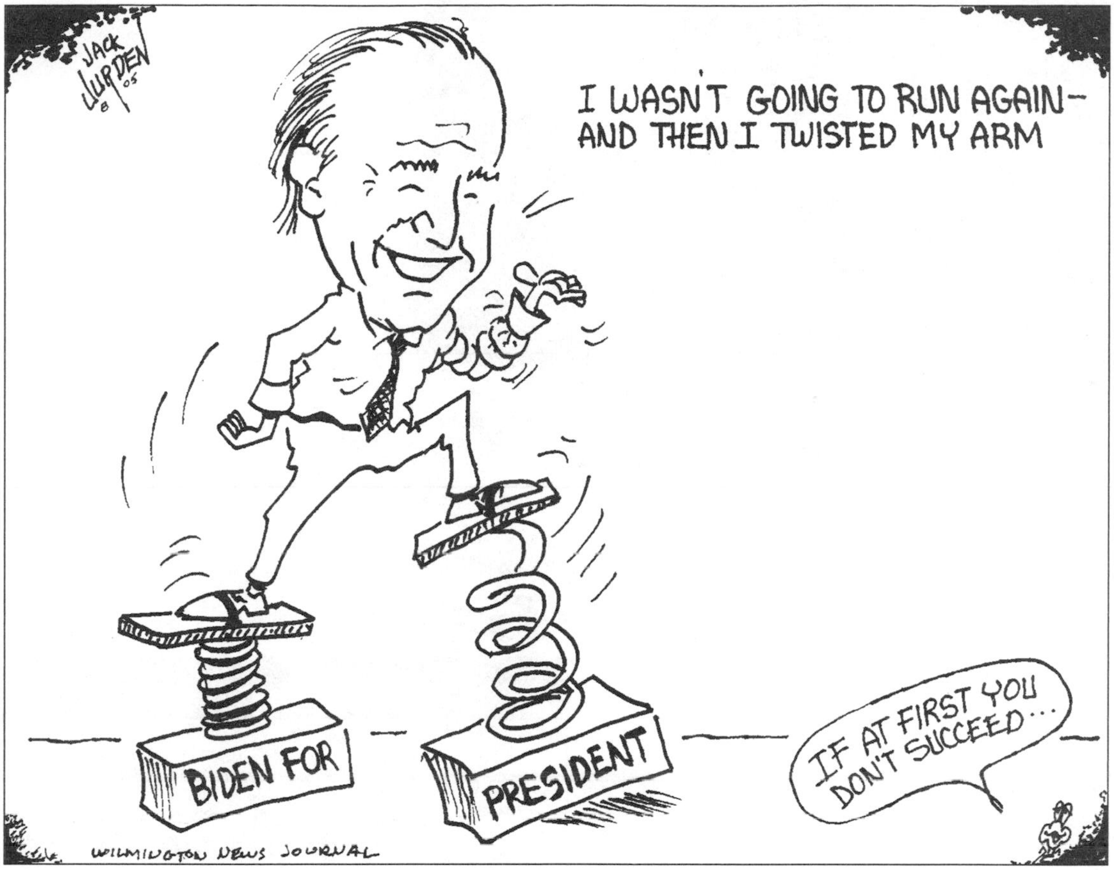
I WASN'T GOING TO RUN AGAIN-
AND THEN I TWISTED MY ARM
BIDEN FOR
PRESIDENT
IF AT FIRST YOU DON'T SUCCEED...
WILMINGTON NEWS JOURNAL

SCOTT STANTIS
Courtesy Birmingham News

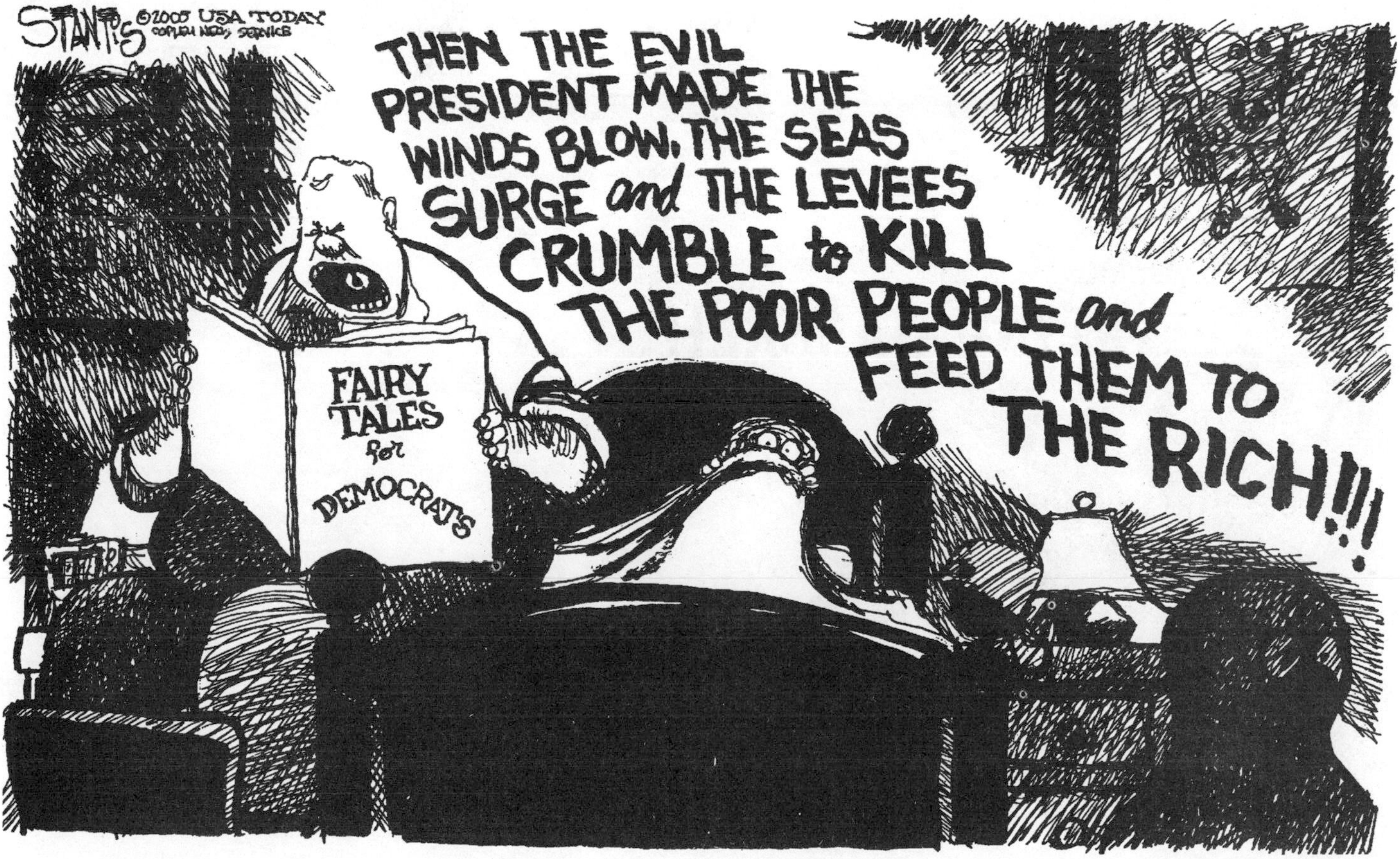
THEN THE EVIL PRESIDENT MADE THE WINDS BLOW, THE SEAS SURGE and THE LEVEES CRUMBLE to KILL THE POOR PEOPLE and FEED THEM TO THE RICH!!!
FAIRY TALES for DEMOCRATS

BRUCE BEATTIE
Courtesy Daytona Beach News-Journal

STEVE EDWARDS
Courtesy St. Louis Journalism Review

ED GAMBLE
Courtesy Florida Times-Union

JOE RANK
Courtesy Rockford Register-Star

DICK LOCHER
Courtesy Chicago Tribune

DAVE SATTLER
Courtesy Lafayette Journal and Courier (Ind.)

NEIL GRAHAME
Courtesy Spencer Newspapers

Society

Connecticut became the second state to legalize civil unions for gay couples and the first to do so without being compelled by the courts. Vermont also allows civil unions, and Massachusetts allows gay couples to marry.

After fifteen years in what doctors called "a persistent vegetative state," Terri Schiavo was allowed to die when a judge ordered her feeding and hydration tubes removed. The case focused national attention on living wills and prompted much of society to examine the issue. The debate continues over what role government should play in such life-and-death situations.

Hoping to reduce the flow of illegal immigration, a group of private citizens calling themselves Minutemen patrolled the border with Mexico and reported what they saw to authorities. Some observers, however, objected to the presence of the Minutemen, contending their actions were racially motivated and interfered with law enforcement efforts.

Recruitment in the armed forces slowed during the year, adding to concerns at the Pentagon. The de-emphasis of religion in schools and society in general seemed to be an emerging national trend. Some organizations, such as the American Civil Liberties Union, appeared determined to eliminate God from public view.

MICHAEL RAMIREZ
Courtesy Los Angeles Times

S. C. RAWLS
Courtesy Rockdale Citizen

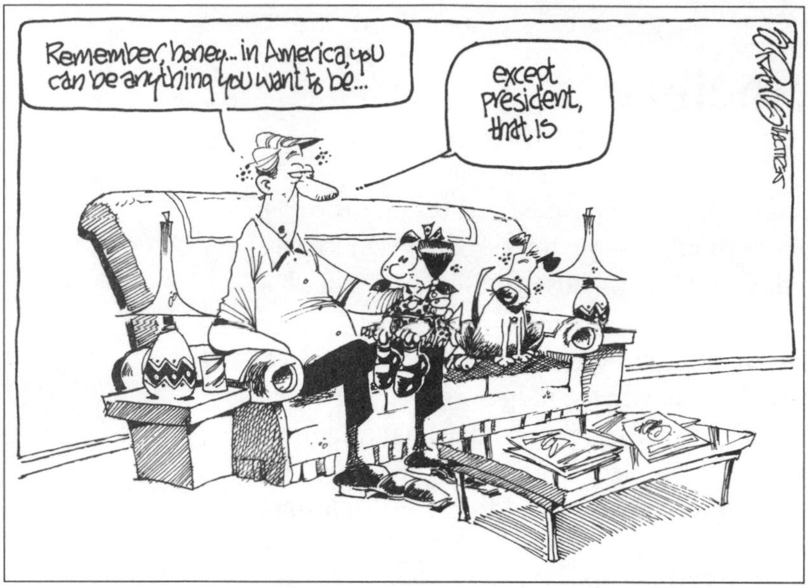
Remember, honey... in America, you can be anything you want to be...
except president, that is

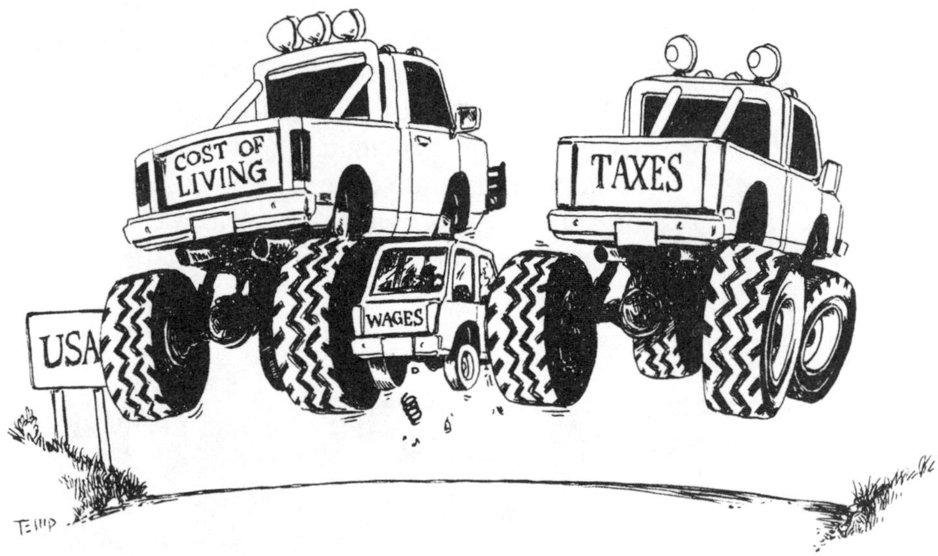
COST OF LIVING
TAXES
WAGES
USA

STEPHEN TEMPLETON
Courtesy The Observer-Times (Pa.)

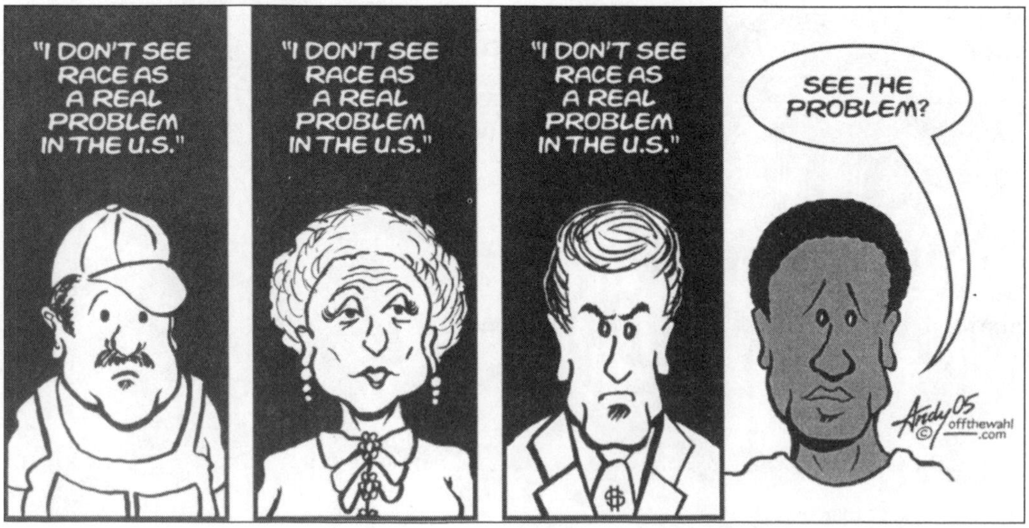
"I DON'T SEE RACE AS A REAL PROBLEM IN THE U.S."
"I DON'T SEE RACE AS A REAL PROBLEM IN THE U.S."
"I DON'T SEE RACE AS A REAL PROBLEM IN THE U.S."
SEE THE PROBLEM?

ANDREW WAHL
Courtesy Wenatchee World

JIM HUNT
Courtesy Charlotte Post

WAYNE STAYSKAL
Courtesy Tribune Media Services

PETER EVANS
Courtesy Islander News (Fla.)

LINDA BOILEAU
Courtesy Frankfort State Journal

ANN CLEAVES
Courtesy Palisadian-Post

JOE HELLER
Courtesy Green Bay Press-Gazette

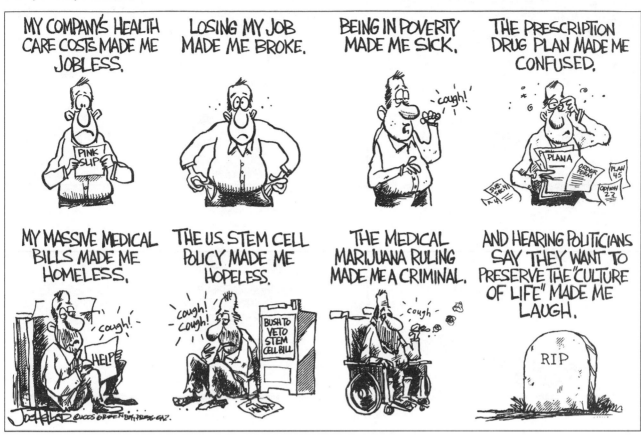

WAYNE STAYSKAL
Courtesy Tribune Media Services

SAM TORODE
Courtesy Books & Culture Journal

THEO MOUDAKIS
Courtesy Toronto Star

STEVE YORK
Courtesy Kankakee Daily Journal

IRENE JOSLIN
Courtesy Brown County Democrat of
Southern Indiana

JOE HELLER
Courtesy Green Bay Press-Gazette

PATRICK O'CONNOR
Courtesy Los Angeles Daily News

DAVE SATTLER
Courtesy Lafayette Journal and Courier (Ind.)

JOEL PETT
Courtesy Lexington Herald-Leader

JOE HELLER
Courtesy Green Bay Press-Gazette

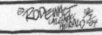

CANADA'S ROLE IN THE NORTH AMERICAN MISSILE SHIELD..

(U.S. closes border to Canadian beef after
Mad Cow Disease scare)

Canada

Canadian immigration authorities reported receiving ten times the normal number of hits on their websites immediately after President Bush's re-election. As many as 150,000 contacts came from the United States in a single day.

Canada's biggest disagreement with the United States centered on tariffs for Canadian softwood lumber. In the wake of the outbreak of Mad Cow Disease, the U.S. closed the border to Canadian beef, and Prime Minister Paul Martin paid a visit to Bush at his Texas ranch.

Volume one of an investigation into the transfer of tax money to Quebec advertising agencies was released to the public. The funds were used to advertise the idea of Canadian unity in Quebec, but a sizeable sum allegedly was funneled to the Quebec Liberal Party for campaign purposes and under-the-table deals.

The scandal shook Canada's government and led to a no-confidence vote in the House of Commons in late November. The vote toppled Prime Minister Martin's minority government and set the stage for new elections early in 2006.

Secretary of State Condoleezza Rice deferred plans for an official visit to Canada after Ottawa decided to opt out of a U.S.-led anti-ballistic missile shield program.

MALCOLM MAYES
Courtesy Edmonton Journal

ROY PETERSON
Courtesy Vancouver Sun

STEVE NEASE
Courtesy Toronto Sun

STEVE NEASE
Courtesy Toronto Sun

STEVE NEASE
Courtesy Toronto Sun

ROY PETERSON
Courtesy Vancouver Sun

MIKE GRASTON
Courtesy Windsor Star

STEVE NEASE
Courtesy London Free Press

VANCE RODEWALT
Courtesy Calgary Herald

MALCOLM MAYES
Courtesy Edmonton Journal

... and Other Issues

After several years of failing health, Pope John Paul II died at age 84. Millions of the faithful flooded Rome to pay their respects. His successor is Pope Benedict XVI. Civil rights heroine Rosa Parks also died during the year. She gained fame in the 1960s by refusing to give up her seat in the front of a Montgomery, Alabama, bus.

Religious broadcaster Pat Robertson came under fire for suggesting on the air that the U.S. should consider assassinating Venezuelan President Hugo Chavez to stop his country from becoming "a launching pad for communist infiltration and Muslim extremism."

Military recruitment lagged, some states wanted to add the concept of "intelligent design" to classroom science discussions, and Cindy Sheehan, the mother of a soldier killed in Iraq, led anti-war demonstrations near President Bush's ranch in Crawford.

In a controversial new interpretation of eminent domain, the U.S. Supreme Court decreed that a citizen's private property could be confiscated if government decides redevelopment would enhance tax revenues.

Newsweek provoked rioting in the Muslim world when it claimed—falsely—that a copy of the Koran had been flushed down a toilet at the U.S. military base in Guantanamo.

MARSHALL RAMSEY
Courtesy The Clarion-Ledger (Miss.)

181

DON LANDGREN JR.
Courtesy The Landmark

ELIZABETH BRICQUET
Courtesy Kingsport Times-News

RICHARD WALLMEYER
Courtesy Long Beach Press-Telegram

PEDRO MOLINA
Courtesy CWS

JAKE FULLER
Courtesy Gainesville Sun

MIKE LUCKOVICH
Courtesy Atlanta Journal-Constitution

JACK HIGGINS
Courtesy Chicago Sun-Times

WAYNE STAYSKAL
Courtesy Tribune Media Services

JESSE SPRINGER
Courtesy Eugene Register-Guard

NICK ANDERSON
Courtesy Louisville Courier-Journal

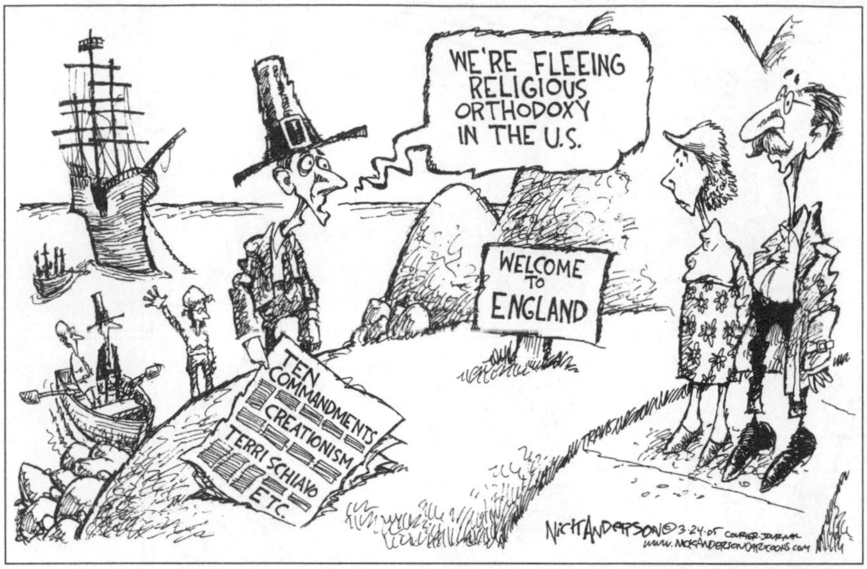
WE'RE FLEEING RELIGIOUS ORTHODOXY IN THE U.S.
WELCOME TO ENGLAND
TEN COMMANDMENTS
CREATIONISM
TERRI SCHIAVO
ETC.
NICK ANDERSON © 3·24·05 COURIER-JOURNAL
www.NICKANDERSONCARTOONS.com

JAMES McCLOSKEY
Courtesy The News Leader (Va.)

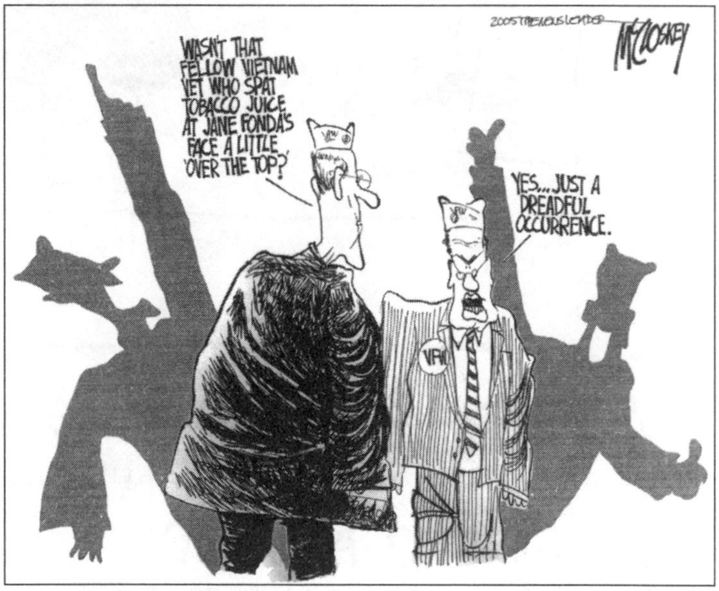
2005 THE NEWS LEADER
McCLOSKEY
WASN'T THAT FELLOW VIETNAM VET WHO SPAT TOBACCO JUICE AT JANE FONDA'S FACE A LITTLE 'OVER THE TOP?'
YES... JUST A DREADFUL OCCURRENCE.
VFW

AN HISTORICAL FIRST

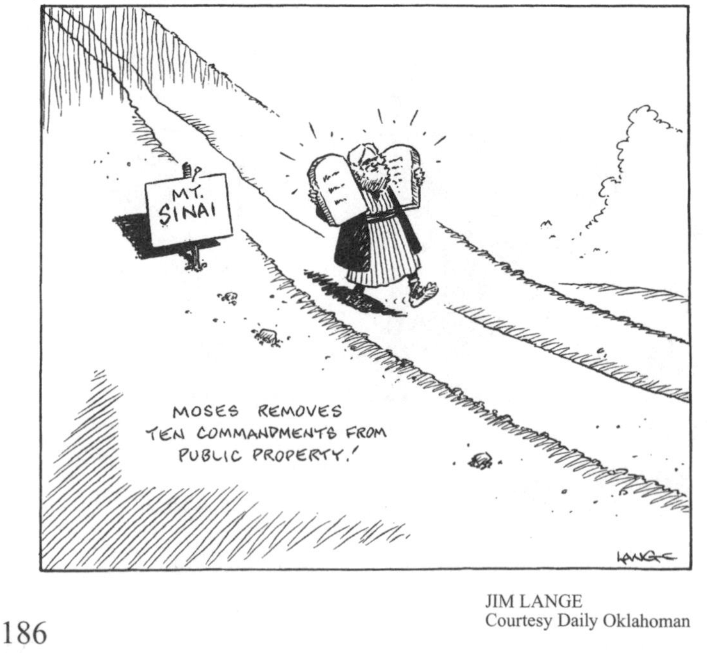
MT. SINAI
MOSES REMOVES TEN COMMANDMENTS FROM PUBLIC PROPERTY!
LANGE

JIM LANGE
Courtesy Daily Oklahoman

SCOTT STANTIS
Courtesy Birmingham News

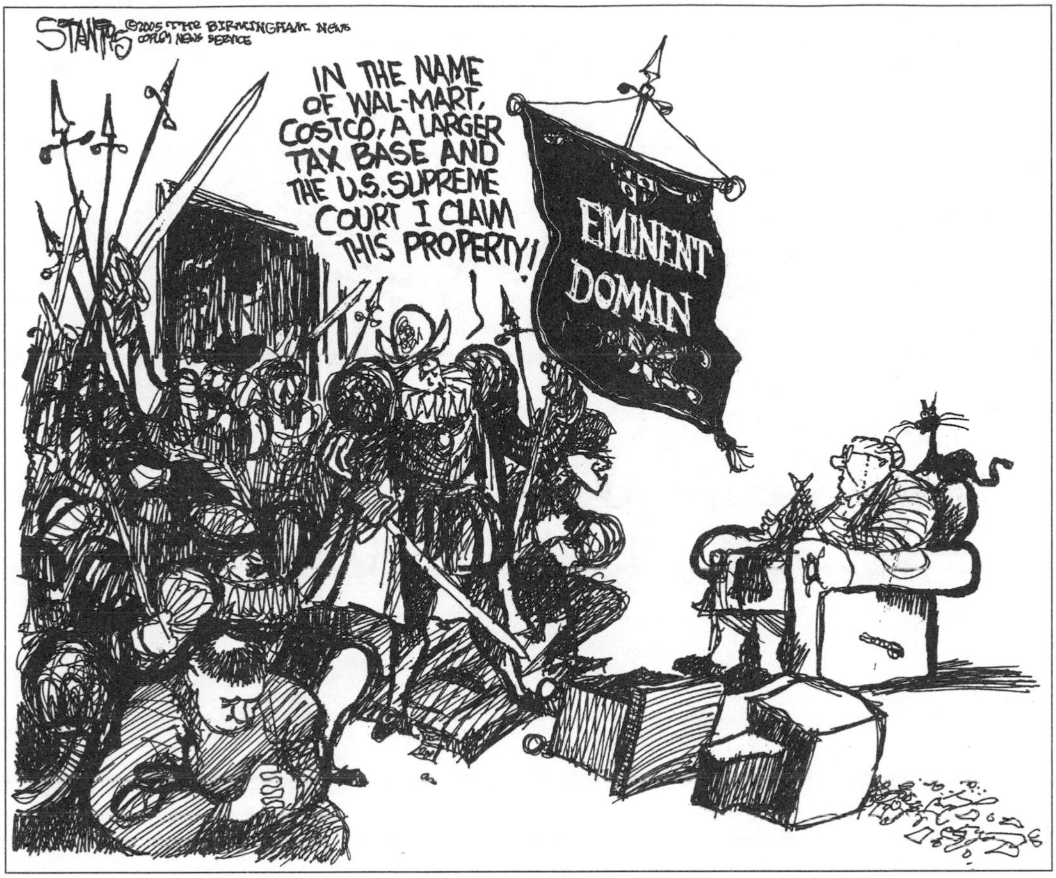
STANTIS
IN THE NAME OF WAL-MART, COSTCO, A LARGER TAX BASE AND THE U.S. SUPREME COURT I CLAIM THIS PROPERTY!
EMINENT DOMAIN

JOHN DEERING
Courtesy Arkansas Democrat-Gazette

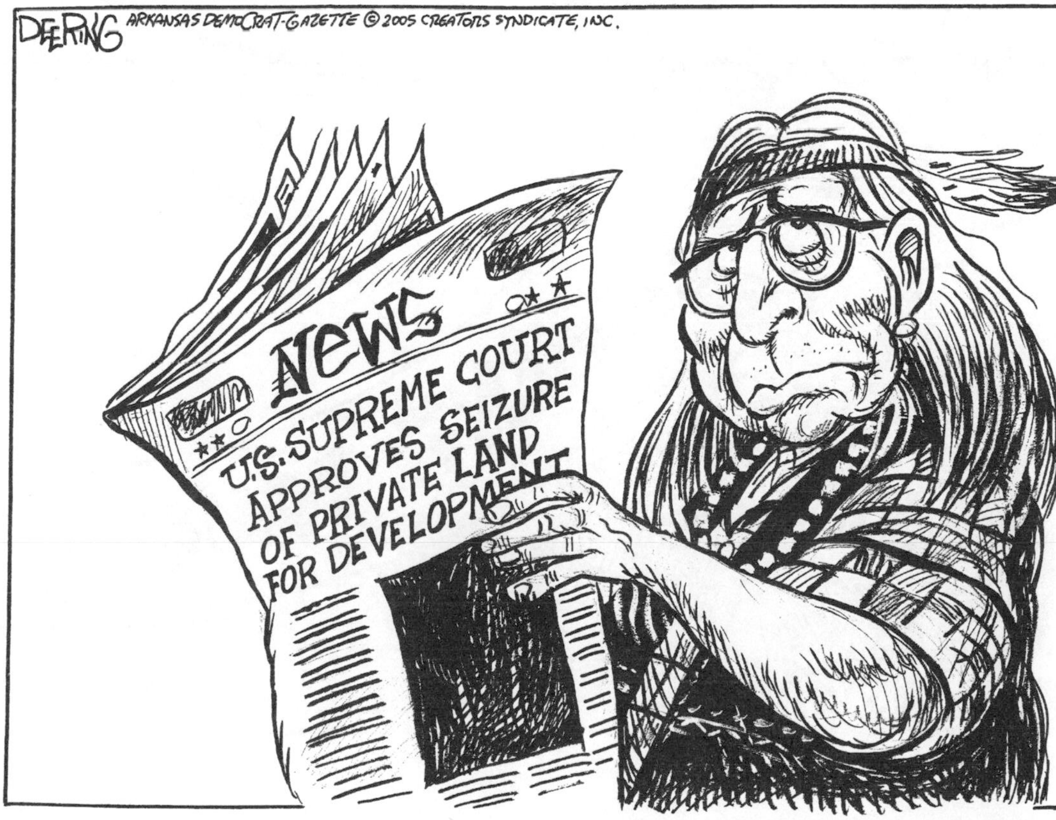
DEERING ARKANSAS DEMOCRAT-GAZETTE © 2005 CREATORS SYNDICATE, INC.
NEWS
U.S. SUPREME COURT APPROVES SEIZURE OF PRIVATE LAND FOR DEVELOPMENT

TOM BECK
Courtesy Freeport Journal-Standard (Ill.)

JOE MAJESKI
Courtesy Wilkes-Barre Times-Leader

ROB SMITH JR.
Courtesy DBR Media

JOHN DEERING
Courtesy Arkansas Democrat-Gazette

JIM BORGMAN
Courtesy Cincinnati Enquirer

189

DAVID COX
Courtesy Arkansas Democrat-Gazette

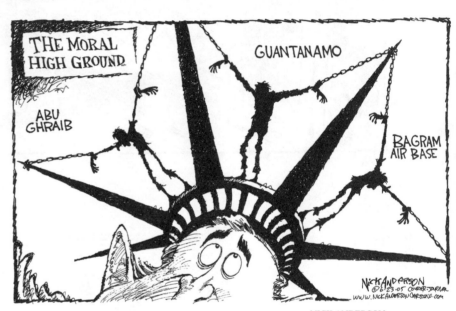

NICK ANDERSON
Courtesy Louisville Courier-Journal

TOM STIGLICH
Courtesy The Northeast Times (Pa.)

JIMMY MARGULIES
Courtesy The Record (N.J.)

JEFF PARKER
Courtesy Florida Today

ED HALL
Courtesy Baker County Press

STEVEN LAIT
Courtesy Oakland Tribune

192

STEVE KELLEY
Courtesy The Times-Picayune (La.)

DICK LOCHER
Courtesy Chicago Tribune

FRED MULHEARN
Courtesy The Advocate (La.)

ANN CLEAVES
Courtesy Palisadian-Post

JACK JURDEN
Courtesy Wilmington News-Journal

CHAN LOWE
Courtesy Fort Lauderdale News/
South Florida Sun-Sentinel

J. R. ROSE
Courtesy Byrd Newspapers of Virginia

ED GAMBLE
Courtesy Florida Times-Union

ETTA HULME
Courtesy Ft. Worth Star-Telegram

STEVE GREENBERG
Courtesy Ventura County Star

JEFF DANZIGER
Courtesy NYTS/CWS

CHUCK ASAY
Courtesy Colorado Springs Gazette-Telegraph

MICHAEL RAMIREZ
Courtesy Los Angeles Times

198

MICHAEL THOMPSON
Detroit Free Press

CHRIS BRITT
Courtesy State Journal-Register (Ill.)

ROGER HARVELL
Courtesy Greenville News-Piedmont

JIM DYKE
Courtesy Jefferson City News-Tribune

ED GAMBLE
Courtesy Florida Times-Union

BILL MANGOLD
Courtesy Heritage Newspapers

CHRIS BRITT
Courtesy State Journal-Register (Ill.)

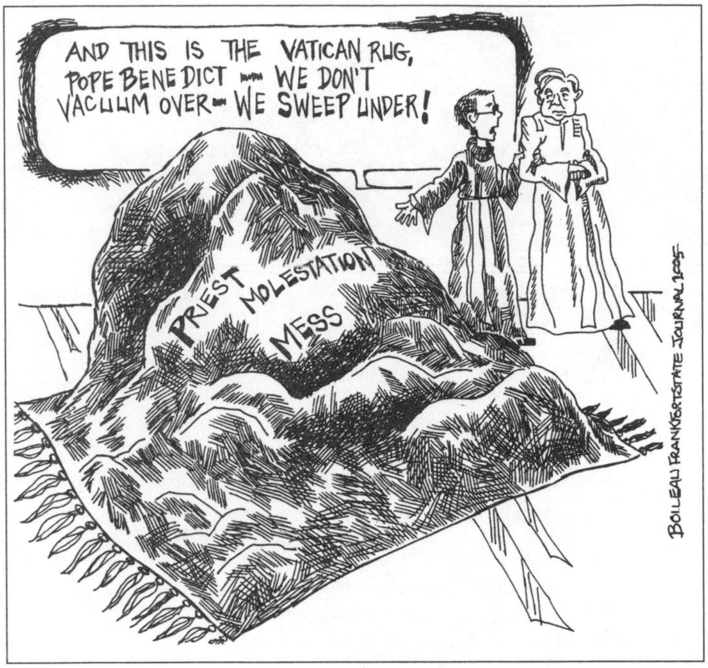
AND THIS IS THE VATICAN RUG, POPE BENEDICT — WE DON'T VACUUM OVER — WE SWEEP UNDER!
PRIEST MOLESTATION MESS

LINDA BOILEAU
Courtesy Frankfort State Journal

STEVE NEASE
Courtesy Toronto Sun

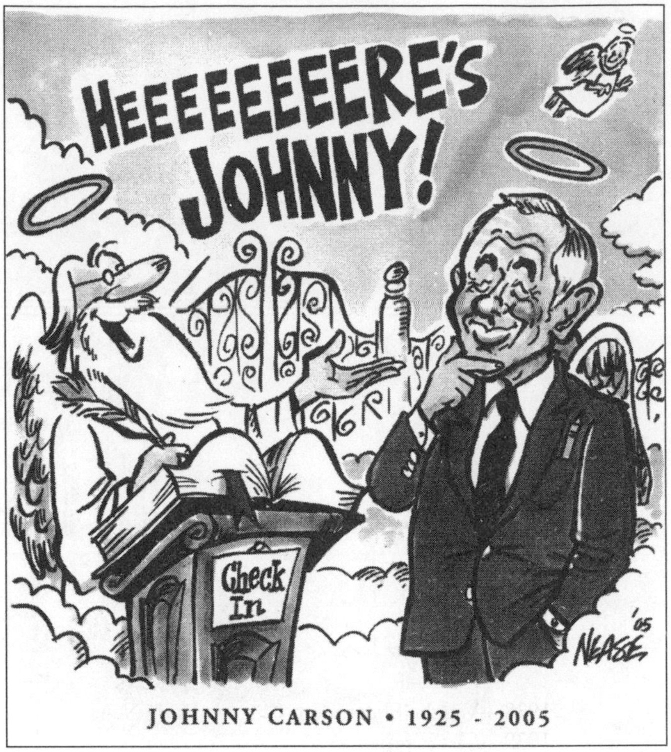
HEEEEEEEERE'S JOHNNY!
Check In
NEASE '05
JOHNNY CARSON • 1925 - 2005

STEVE BREEN
Courtesy San Diego Union-Tribune

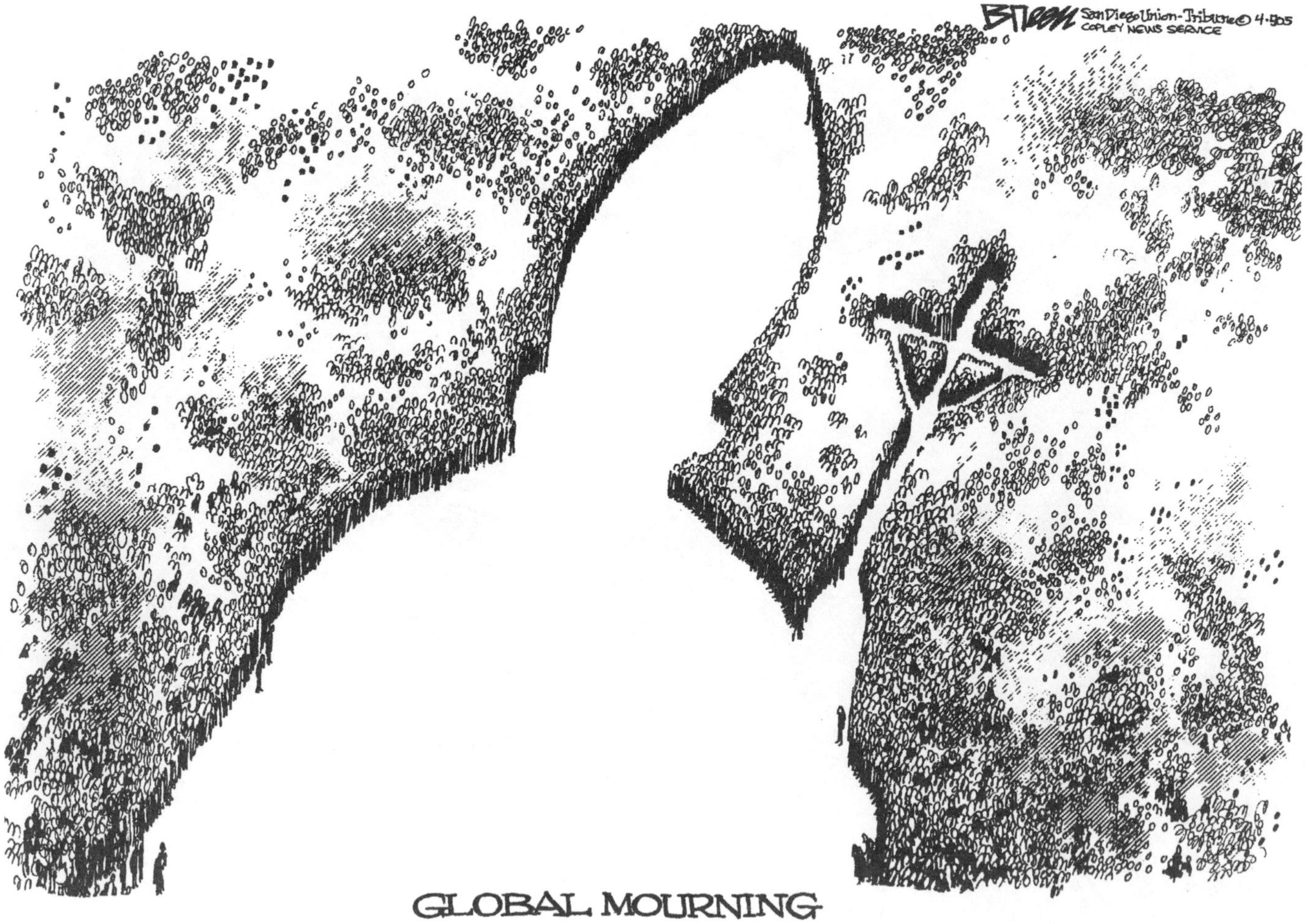
COPLEY NEWS SERVICE
GLOBAL MOURNING

Past Award Winners

PULITZER PRIZE

1922—Rollin Kirby, New York World
1923—No award given
1924—J.N. Darling, New York Herald-Tribune
1925—Rollin Kirby, New York World
1926—D.R. Fitzpatrick, St. Louis Post-Dispatch
1927—Nelson Harding, Brooklyn Eagle
1928—Nelson Harding, Brooklyn Eagle
1929—Rollin Kirby, New York World
1930—Charles Macauley, Brooklyn Eagle
1931—Edmund Duffy, Baltimore Sun
1932—John T. McCutcheon, Chicago Tribune
1933—H.M. Talburt, Washington Daily News
1934—Edmund Duffy, Baltimore Sun
1935—Ross A. Lewis, Milwaukee Journal
1936—No award given
1937—C.D. Batchelor, New York Daily News
1938—Vaughn Shoemaker, Chicago Daily News
1939—Charles G. Werner, Daily Oklahoman
1940—Edmund Duffy, Baltimore Sun
1941—Jacob Burck, Chicago Times
1942—Herbert L. Block, NEA
1943—Jay N. Darling, New York Herald-Tribune
1944—Clifford K. Berryman, Washington Star
1945—Bill Mauldin, United Features Syndicate
1946—Bruce Russell, Los Angeles Times
1947—Vaughn Shoemaker, Chicago Daily News
1948—Reuben L. ("Rube") Goldberg, New York Sun
1949—Lute Pease, Newark Evening News
1950—James T. Berryman, Washington Star
1951—Reginald W. Manning, Arizona Republic
1952—Fred L. Packer, New York Mirror
1953—Edward D. Kuekes, Cleveland Plain Dealer
1954—Herbert L. Block, Washington Post
1955—Daniel R. Fitzpatrick, St. Louis Post-Dispatch
1956—Robert York, Louisville Times
1957—Tom Little, Nashville Tennessean
1958—Bruce M. Shanks, Buffalo Evening News
1959—Bill Mauldin, St. Louis Post-Dispatch
1960—No award given
1961—Carey Orr, Chicago Tribune
1962—Edmund S. Valtman, Hartford Times
1963—Frank Miller, Des Moines Register
1964—Paul Conrad, Denver Post
1965—No award given
1966—Don Wright, Miami News
1967—Patrick B. Oliphant, Denver Post
1968—Eugene Gray Payne, Charlotte Observer
1969—John Fischetti, Chicago Daily News
1970—Thomas F. Darcy, Newsday
1971—Paul Conrad, Los Angeles Times
1972—Jeffrey K. MacNelly, Richmond News Leader
1973—No award given
1974—Paul Szep, Boston Globe
1975—Garry Trudeau, Universal Press Syndicate

1976—Tony Auth, Philadelphia Enquirer
1977—Paul Szep, Boston Globe
1978—Jeff MacNelly, Richmond News Leader
1979—Herbert Block, Washington Post
1980—Don Wright, Miami News
1981—Mike Peters, Dayton Daily News
1982—Ben Sargent, Austin American-Statesman
1983—Dick Locher, Chicago Tribune
1984—Paul Conrad, Los Angeles Times
1985—Jeff MacNelly, Chicago Tribune
1986—Jules Feiffer, Universal Press Syndicate
1987—Berke Breathed, Washington Post Writers Group
1988—Doug Marlette, Atlanta Constitution
1989—Jack Higgins, Chicago Sun-Times
1990—Tom Toles, Buffalo News
1991—Jim Borgman, Cincinnati Enquirer
1992—Signe Wilkinson, Philadelphia Daily News
1993—Steve Benson, Arizona Republic
1994—Michael Ramirez, Memphis Commercial Appeal
1995—Mike Luckovich, Atlanta Constitution
1996—Jim Morin, Miami Herald
1997—Walt Handelsman, New Orleans Times-Picayune
1998—Steve Breen, Asbury Park Press
1999—David Horsey, Seattle Post-Intelligencer
2000—Joel Pett, Lexington Herald-Leader
2001—Ann Telnaes, Tribune Media Services
2002—Clay Bennett, Christian Science Monitor
2003—David Horsey, Seattle Post-Intelligencer
2004—Matt Davies, The Journal News
2005—Nick Anderson, Louisville Courier-Journal

NATIONAL SOCIETY OF PROFESSIONAL JOURNALISTS AWARD (SIGMA DELTA CHI AWARD)

1942—Jacob Burck, Chicago Times
1943—Charles Werner, Chicago Sun
1944—Henry Barrow, Associated Press
1945—Reuben L. Goldberg, New York Sun
1946—Dorman H. Smith, NEA
1947—Bruce Russell, Los Angeles Times
1948—Herbert Block, Washington Post
1949—Herbert Block, Washington Post
1950—Bruce Russell, Los Angeles Times
1951—Herbert Block, Washington Post and
      Bruce Russell, Los Angeles Times
1952—Cecil Jensen, Chicago Daily News
1953—John Fischetti, NEA
1954—Calvin Alley, Memphis Commercial Appeal
1955—John Fischetti, NEA
1956—Herbert Block, Washington Post
1957—Scott Long, Minneapolis Tribune
1958—Clifford H. Baldowski, Atlanta Constitution

PAST AWARD WINNERS

1959—Charles G. Brooks, Birmingham News
1960—Dan Dowling, New York Herald-Tribune
1961—Frank Interlandi, Des Moines Register
1962—Paul Conrad, Denver Post
1963—William Mauldin, Chicago Sun-Times
1964—Charles Bissell, Nashville Tennessean
1965—Roy Justus, Minneapolis Star
1966—Patrick Oliphant, Denver Post
1967—Eugene Payne, Charlotte Observer
1968—Paul Conrad, Los Angeles Times
1969—William Mauldin, Chicago Sun-Times
1970—Paul Conrad, Los Angeles Times
1971—Hugh Haynie, Louisville Courier-Journal
1972—William Mauldin, Chicago Sun-Times
1973—Paul Szep, Boston Globe
1974—Mike Peters, Dayton Daily News
1975—Tony Auth, Philadelphia Enquirer
1976—Paul Szep, Boston Globe
1977—Don Wright, Miami News
1978—Jim Borgman, Cincinnati Enquirer
1979—John P. Trever, Albuquerque Journal
1980—Paul Conrad, Los Angeles Times
1981—Paul Conrad, Los Angeles Times

1982—Dick Locher, Chicago Tribune
1983—Rob Lawlor, Philadelphia Daily News
1984—Mike Lane, Baltimore Evening Sun
1985—Doug Marlette, Charlotte Observer
1986—Mike Keefe, Denver Post
1987—Paul Conrad, Los Angeles Times
1988—Jack Higgins, Chicago Sun-Times
1989—Don Wright, Palm Beach Post
1990—Jeff MacNelly, Chicago Tribune
1991—Walt Handelsman, New Orleans Times-Picayune
1992—Robert Ariail, Columbia State
1993—Herbert Block, Washington Post
1994—Jim Borgman, Cincinnati Enquirer
1995—Michael Ramirez, Memphis Commercial Appeal
1996—Paul Conrad, Los Angeles Times
1997—Michael Ramirez, Los Angeles Times
1998—Jack Higgins, Chicago Sun-Times
1999—Mike Thompson, Detroit Free Press
2000—Nick Anderson, Louisville Courier-Journal
2001—Clay Bennett, Christian Science Monitor
2002—Mike Thompson, Detroit Free Press
2003—Steve Sack, Minneapolis Star-Tribune
2004—John Sherffius, jsherffius@aol.com

Index of Cartoonists

INDEX OF CARTOONISTS

Complete Your CARTOON COLLECTION

Previous editions of this timeless classic are available for those wishing to update their collection of the most provocative moments of the past three decades. In the early days the topics were the oil crisis, Richard Nixon's presidency, Watergate, and the Vietnam War. Those subjects have given way to the Clinton impeachment trial, the historic 2000 presidential election, and the terrorist attack on America. Most important, in the end, the wit and wisdom of the editorial cartoonists prevail on the pages of these op-ed editorials, where one can find memories and much, much more in the work of the nation's finest cartoonists.

Select from the following supply of past editions

_____ 1972 Edition $20.00 pb (F)	_____ 1985 Edition $20.00 pb (F)	_____ 1997 Edition $20.00 pb
_____ 1974 Edition $20.00 pb (F)	_____ 1986 Edition $20.00 pb (F)	_____ 1998 Edition $20.00 pb
_____ 1975 Edition $20.00 pb (F)	_____ 1987 Edition $20.00 pb	_____ 1999 Edition $20.00 pb
_____ 1976 Edition $20.00 pb (F)	_____ 1988 Edition $20.00 pb	_____ 2000 Edition $20.00 pb
_____ 1977 Edition $20.00 pb (F)	_____ 1989 Edition $20.00 pb (F)	_____ 2001 Edition $20.00 pb
_____ 1978 Edition $20.00 pb (F)	_____ 1990 Edition $20.00 pb	_____ 2002 Edition $14.95 pb
_____ 1979 Edition $20.00 pb (F)	_____ 1991 Edition $20.00 pb	_____ 2003 Edition $14.95 pb
_____ 1980 Edition $20.00 pb (F)	_____ 1992 Edition $20.00 pb	_____ 2004 Edition $14.95 pb
_____ 1981 Edition $20.00 pb (F)	_____ 1993 Edition $20.00 pb	_____ 2005 Edition $14.95 pb
_____ 1982 Edition $20.00 pb (F)	_____ 1994 Edition $20.00 pb	_____ 2006 Edition $14.95 pb
_____ 1983 Edition $20.00 pb (F)	_____ 1995 Edition $20.00 pb	_____ Add me to the list of standing
_____ 1984 Edition $20.00 pb (F)	_____ 1996 Edition $20.00 pb	orders

Please include $2.95 for 4th Class Postage and handling or $6.85 for UPS Ground Shipment plus $.75 for each additional copy ordered.

Total enclosed: _____

NAME _____

ADDRESS _____

CITY_____STATE_____ZIP_____

Make checks payable to:

PELICAN PUBLISHING COMPANY
1000 Burmaster St, Dept. 6BEC
Gretna, Louisiana 70053-2246